VEGETARIAN COOKBOOK FOR TEENS

Vegetarian Cookbook

FOR

Teens

Sarah Baker

ROCKRIDGE
PRESS

Interior and Cover Designer: Francesca Pacchini
Art Producer: Michael Hardgrove
Editor: Adrian Potts
Production Editor: Andrew Yackira

Photography © 2020 Annie Martin. Food styling by Oscar Molinar, cover, pp. ii, x, 14, 22, 27, 36, 52, 72, 100, 115, 132, 141, 154; Shutterstock/Kyselova Inna, p. vi; Shutterstock/Jiri Hera, p. ix; Shutterstock/Ludmila Ivashchenko, p. 3; Shutterstock/Piotr Debowski, p. 4; Shutterstock/Hein Nouwens, pp. 5, 6, 7; Shutterstock/New Africa, p. 11; Shutterstock/Anna Kucherova, p. 12.

ISBN: Print 978-1-64611-903-5 | eBook 978-1-64611-904-2

R0

To my son, Christian, who I hope one day
will find this book useful.

INTRODUCTION

COOKING IS ONE OF THE MOST IMPORTANT life skills you will need as you grow up, but it is even more essential if you are a vegetarian. Whether you're new to this way of eating or not, you may currently be picking around the meat dishes your family serves up, or attempting to make a full meal out of vegetable side dishes. Both scenarios can feel frustrating. This book will help you create your very own vegetarian meals and grow into a full-fledged vegetarian cooking expert!

Nothing is better than being independent, right? Your parents will be extra proud of your independence in the kitchen and the responsibility you are showing with your chosen way of eating. YOU are taking charge now to become more in control of what you eat. The recipes in this book may even encourage your parents and siblings to eat more meatless meals so the whole family can join in.

In my own life, I have been able to channel my passion for food and well-being into my work as a certified plant-based and integrative nutrition consultant, a certified holistic health coach, and the founder of BalancedBabe.com. I launched the site in 2012 as a platform to provide realistic and approachable guides for healthy living and, most importantly, healthy eating. I am passionate about educating people on how easy it can be to cook vegetarian meals, and I also have a kiddo who I hope will one day learn a trick or two from this book.

Whether you are full-blown vegetarian or just curious about adding more meatless meals to your diet, you will learn to cook recipes that will fill you up and satisfy your taste buds. Whatever your reason for exploring vegetarian cooking—being kind to animals, reducing your carbon footprint, and/or enjoying the health benefits of eating more plants—this book will show you that vegetarian cooking does not have to mean eating boring sprouts and salads. Vegetarian cooking is a fun, flavorful, and easy skill to master!

MEDITERRANEAN
PITA, PAGE 83

chapter 1
YOU'RE THE CHEF

REGARDLESS OF YOUR EXPERIENCE IN THE KITCHEN, YOU are now about to learn everything you need to know to become an expert vegetarian chef. This book will help you gain cooking confidence in the kitchen with step-by-step guidance, teaching you everything from how to create a flavorful breakfast burrito in 10 minutes flat to how to simmer up a hearty vegetarian chili with your own creative twist.

In this chapter, you will learn about various types of cooking techniques and the most common cooking terms—like the difference between boiling and simmering—so that you can easily make all the recipes in this book. This chapter also serves as a reference section for various cooking tools you'll want to have on hand.

Additionally, I'll explain some of the benefits of eating vegetarian in this chapter. You will learn about the many advantages of incorporating certain plant-based foods into your meals, including the vital nutrients they provide, and I'll give you some tips on handling tricky questions about your choice to follow a plant-based diet. Let's get started!

Kitchen Basics

Knowing where to begin when it comes to cooking your own meals may seem intimidating, but there is no need to stress. This section outlines how to set up your kitchen space for cooking success. From preparing yourself and your space to knowing what kitchen tools to have on hand and how to use them, you'll learn exactly what you need to start whipping up the recipes in this book.

Getting Set Up

The first step chefs take when getting to work is setting up their space. After selecting the recipe you want to make, take a look around your kitchen to see what ingredients you already have on hand. If you are missing any specific ingredients, make a shopping list and tag along with your parents to the grocery store, if you can.

Once you are back in the kitchen, make sure you are prepared to cook. If you have long hair, tie it back so that it does not end up in your food. Protect your clothing from sticky ingredients and stains from spices and oils by donning an apron. Once you are decked out in your chef attire, lay out all the ingredients and utensils your recipe calls for.

If you are following a recipe that requires specific measurements of ingredients, measure these all out now. Prep any ingredients that require extra processing. This will help you stay in the zone as you cook and make your time in the kitchen go more smoothly and quickly.

Cooking 101

To start cooking, you need to understand some common cooking terms so you'll know how to take action in the kitchen.

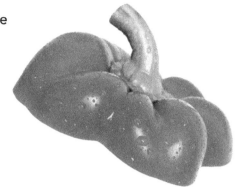

BEAT: Typically done with an electric hand-held mixer or stand mixer, to beat ingredients means to stir them really fast so they blend well together.

BOIL: Boiling food requires a pot filled with water or broth that is heated to reach its boiling point on a stovetop. You will know water is starting to boil once you see what looks like bubbles rolling rapidly to the surface.

BROIL: Broiling cooks food through direct exposure to very high heat, most commonly in the oven when you turn the setting to "broil," but grilling can also create the same effect.

CHOP: While chopping up food into smaller pieces with a knife is fairly self-explanatory, there are a few different techniques you'll come across in this book:

> **Dice:** Dicing takes a bit more focus, as you are cutting your food into small and consistent cubes.

> **Slice:** Slicing cuts your ingredients into slim pieces, like when preparing a sweet potato to make Sweet Potato Fries (page 62).

> **Mince:** This chopping technique results in ultrasmall pieces. The most common ingredient you will be mincing is garlic.

GREASE: When cooking or baking food in an oven, you will normally need to grease your pan or baking sheet with oil to prevent food from sticking to it.

Whoops!

You will most likely make some mistakes as you learn how to cook, and that is completely normal. Blunders in the kitchen are a major part of learning how to make new recipes and fully understanding how to cook. The most skilled and highly trained chefs in the world make mistakes, even after years of practice! What's important is to learn from your missteps so you can do things better next time.

Here are a few common mistakes you may experience while you are making these recipes:

- Not measuring ingredients properly
- Forgetting to set your timer
- Overcooking or burning a meal
- Over- or under-seasoning your food

As mistakes happen, think about what went wrong and how you can approach your recipe differently the next time. As you grow your cooking skills, you may even find yourself creating an entirely new recipe from a mishap!

● **PURÉE:** Puréeing requires a food processor or blender to mash or blend ingredients until they have a smooth consistency free of lumps and bumps.

● **SAUTÉ:** Sautéing involves heating up a skillet, pan, or pot on a stovetop with a bit of fat, like oil or butter, to cook ingredients.

● **SIMMER:** Think of simmering as the gentler version of boiling, where your liquid is "bubbling," but the bubbles are tiny and pop up to the surface more slowly.

● **STEAM:** Steaming requires you to place the food *above* boiling water in a pot. You will need a wire steamer insert to hold ingredients over the boiling water.

● **WHIP:** Even though whipping may seem similar to beating, when you whip ingredients, the goal is to incorporate air, or to make your ingredients "fluffy." This usually requires a whisk and is done by hand (whereas beating usually requires a handheld or stand mixer).

Essential Equipment

To use your newfound cooking skills, you need the right type of kitchen equipment. Many of these items can be used in more than one way and are most likely already in your kitchen.

- **BAKING DISH:** These deep, ceramic or stainless-steel dishes are oven-safe and often used to make casseroles, breads, and other baked recipes, like lasagna.

- **BAKING SHEET:** These are flat, metal sheet pans used for baking, roasting, or broiling food in the oven. They can be used to cook pizzas, cookies, or roasted vegetables.

- **BLENDER:** A blender is used to blend together ingredients to make smoothies, sauces, or any other food that needs to be smooth and well mixed.

- **13-INCH CAST-IRON SKILLET:** Cast-iron skillets are commonly used for cooking on the stove as well as in the oven (since cast iron is oven-safe). Depending on the type you have at home, either it will be precoated with some sort of nonstick surface or it will require you to add an oil coating to it before and after use.

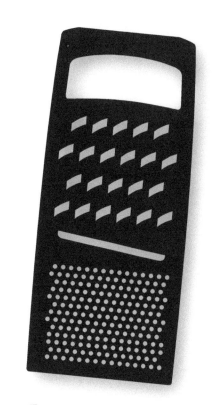

- **CHEESE/HANDHELD GRATER:** This is a metal device that typically shreds cheese into small strips to be spread over dishes. It can also be used to grate other foods, such as zucchini and other starchy vegetables, into fine strands.

- **KNIVES:** Three types of knives are great to have to make meal prep a cinch. I've specified which type is best for different ingredients in each recipe, but if you find yourself short of one of these knives, don't stress. Simply use another

knife you think is best and follow the safety instructions later on in this chapter.

Paring knife: This knife is smaller than a chef's knife, and the blade is straight and short. A paring knife is usually needed when a recipe calls for smaller ingredients, such as minced garlic or fresh herbs cut into small pieces.

Serrated knife: This knife has little edges on the blade that look like teeth. Serrated knives are great for cutting through pies, breads, tomatoes, soft fruits, or any type of food that would be squashed by other types of knives.

Chef's knife: This type of knife is versatile, allowing you to slice, dice, and chop. A chef's knife is a bit heftier than other knives, so that you can cut through thick vegetables, like squash or sweet potatoes.

MEASURING CUPS AND SPOONS: Measuring cups are typically used to measure liquid and solid ingredients, such as nut milks, oils, and flours. Measuring spoons are for measurements of ingredients used in smaller quantities, such as spices.

MIXING BOWLS: These bowls come in different sizes and are used when you need to beat, whip, or mix ingredients together.

NONSTICK PAN: Nonstick pans and skillets have a coating that prevents food from getting stuck to them during the cooking process.

SAUCEPAN: These pans, which are typically metal and made for use on the stovetop, are deep enough to boil water and make sauces and smaller batches of soups and stews. They have a long handle and typically come with a lid.

- **STOCKPOT:** Stockpots are large pots typically used to make larger amounts of soups, stews, and pasta. Stockpots have wide bottoms and tall sides and typically come with a lid.

- **UTENSILS:** You will need a silicone or rubber spatula for mixing and spreading things, a whisk to mix together ingredients in a mixing bowl, and a wooden spoon for stirring recipes like soups, sauces, and stews without scratching your pan's surface.

- **VEGETABLE PEELER:** A vegetable peeler is a small tool that has two sharp metal blades attached to a handle. These blades remove the skin from produce, such as carrots, apples, and potatoes.

Make It Fun

The most important thing to remember while in the kitchen is that cooking should be fun! Once you get the hang of the most common techniques, cooking can become a calming and enjoyable hobby. Here are a few ways to add fun to your cooking:

COOK TO MUSIC. Create a special playlist you can blast in the kitchen to rock out to while you cook.

INVOLVE FRIENDS. Cooking with a buddy can help you complete recipes faster, and you will get a chance to show off your newfound skills.

IMPRESS YOUR FAMILY. Pick a night of the week to make a meatless meal for your family, and give yourself a pat on the back when you see how impressed they are with what you have learned.

FOLLOW YOUR INTUITION. Once you start making a lot of the recipes in this book, you will gain an understanding of which flavors and ingredients go well together. This gives you the opportunity to be creative in coming up with your own recipes. You may be surprised by what you can create on your own!

Safety First

One of the most important things to remember as you start cooking is how to use your tools correctly and safely. Understanding kitchen safety will prevent injuries, like cuts and burns, and illness from germs. If you are unsure of how to use a kitchen tool or need a helping hand chopping produce or using your oven, you can always turn to your parents.

KNIVES

The most important way to stay safe in the kitchen is to understand how to use a knife correctly. Knives are extremely sharp and, when used incorrectly, can lead to injuries. Here are some important ways to protect yourself:

Choose the right knife. Did you know that using sharper knives to chop ingredients is actually safer than using blunt ones? This is because sharp blades cut smoothly with little force or effort, whereas blunt ones take more elbow grease, which could increase your chances of cutting yourself. If your knife seems dull, ask your parents to sharpen it for you.

Protect your fingers. When chopping ingredients, make sure to curl the tips of your fingers under so that they are not exposed to the blade.

Maintain a steady grip. Not only do cutting boards protect your countertop, but they are also essential to helping you keep a steady grip on your knife and the ingredient you are cutting. If your board seems to be a bit slippery on your kitchen counter, put a damp kitchen towel underneath it for extra grip.

Pay attention and take your time. Slow down and make sure you are always completely focused on the task at hand.

Take the right steps to keep yourself safe from burns. First, regardless of whether your stove is electric or has a flame, never touch its surface while it is on. Even once the stove is turned off, it will still be extremely hot for a while. Never wear loose sleeves or any clothing that can catch on fire.

Spatulas and wooden spoons are typically the only utensils that should be used when sautéing, simmering, or boiling food on the stove. And when handling pots and pans that contain boiling water or simmering food, touch only the handles.

When using the oven, always protect your hands with oven mitts. The inside of the oven door will be just as hot as the racks, so take your time when removing dishes.

KEEPING CLEAN

While it's normal for sauces to splash on the counter or a film of flour to coat your working surface or floor, keep the kitchen clean before and after you cook. The first rule of cleanliness is to always wash your hands before and as needed during the cooking process to get rid of any germs. Also, produce, like vegetables and fruits, should always be thoroughly washed and rinsed to get rid of germs, soil particles, and chemicals used in their production.

After cooking, it is important to clean all the equipment you used, including cutting boards, pots, and pans. Even though kitchen counter (and sometimes floor) messes are inevitable, it is important to wipe down the area where you cooked to kill all germs. Bonus: Your parents will be extra happy about this step.

Why It's Green to Go Veggie

Did you know that becoming vegetarian is one of the easiest ways to be kind toward our planet? When you focus on eating plants, you are helping protect the environment in several ways:

- **Lowering greenhouse gases:** By reducing emissions from livestock and animal farming, such as carbon dioxide, methane, and ammonia, which all contribute to global warming.
- **Reducing pollution:** The livestock industry contributes to littering rivers and oceans with animal waste and chemicals. Going vegetarian cuts down on this type of pollution.
- **Saving ridiculously large amounts of water:** You would be amazed at how much water it takes to create meat products.
- **Protecting forests:** Animal farming uses more land than plant-based farming, so a vegetarian diet helps prevent deforestation.

The Healthy Vegetarian

What a truly awesome step you are taking by exploring the world of vegetarianism. When cutting down on animal products in your diet, it is important to know what nutrients to include in your meals to keep you strong, alert, and energized. Luckily, by simply eating more vegetables, fruits, whole grains, dairy, and legumes, you are filling up your plate with a boatload of healthy vitamins and minerals.

Nutrients Made Easy

As a vegetarian teen, you need to take a little extra care to make sure you are getting all the right nutrients. But don't worry, there are plenty of vegetarian superfoods to help you achieve a perfectly balanced diet.

Protein: Now that you are not eating meat, you may be wondering where your protein is coming from. Thankfully, there are many plant-based sources of protein, such as tofu, legumes, lentils, quinoa, seitan, oatmeal, wild rice, nuts and nut butter, and some vegetables, like broccoli, spinach, and sweet potatoes.

Iron: This mineral boosts your energy and athletic performance. Girls in particular need to be aware of getting enough iron, since they lose some during menstruation. If you think you may need to supplement with iron, do not hesitate to speak with your doctor. Iron-rich foods include certain vegetables, like collard greens, Swiss chard, and sun-dried tomatoes; nuts, like pistachios and cashews; and legumes, like white beans, black beans, and tofu.

Calcium: This mineral supports the superfast growth you are going through by helping your bones grow extra strong. It also supports hormones and other parts of your body that change as you grow. If you love dairy, you can get it from yogurt (especially Greek yogurt, which also contains great amounts of protein); cheeses, like paneer, mozzarella, and feta; and of course, milk. If you are not a fan of dairy, you can find calcium in tofu, dried apricots, kale, cabbage, broccoli, fortified nut milks, almond butter, chickpeas, and pinto beans.

Vitamin B$_{12}$: This vitamin is extra important, as it plays a big role in how your body functions by supporting healthy blood levels, brain health, and even your mood. Great sources of vitamin B$_{12}$ include yogurt, milk, eggs, shiitake mushrooms, and fortified cereals.

Omega-3: This is a healthy fat that supports brain health, may fend off anxiety and depression, and helps your hair, skin, and nails grow strong. Excellent sources of omega-3 include chia seeds, walnuts, flaxseed, edamame, and kidney beans.

Dealing with Tricky Questions

As you start embracing a vegetarian lifestyle, you may get questions from friends and family. More often than not, you will be surrounded by super supportive people who are cheering you on. However, you may also encounter questions from time to time that might make you feel put on the spot. Lucky for you, you can use a few of the following easy responses to avoid awkward conversations.

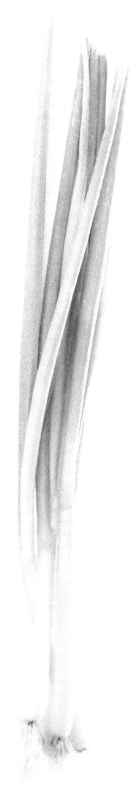

Why are you a vegetarian? When someone asks you this, remember that it is your life and decision. You can elaborate on your personal choice if you feel comfortable, explaining your love of animals or care for the environment, for example. But if you don't feel like going into it, you can simply say, "I just feel better this way," and change the topic.

Can't you just pick out the meat? Simply decline politely and opt to fill up on the side dishes instead.

Should I make something special for you? For special events and holidays, the host may ask if they should make something special for you. Depending on the relationship between you and the host, you can suggest an easy vegetarian option to make, or you can reassure them that any plant-based sides and appetizers will fill you up. Alternately, you may be inspired to offer to bring a dish you cooked from this book.

Can't you take a joke? There may be people in your life who don't fully understand why somebody would be a vegetarian and may joke about your choice. Most of the time, these jokes are filled with good intent. Brush it off and remember that they are joking only because they are unaware of the benefits of a vegetarian diet. Eventually, they will run out of jokes and it will be old news.

About These Recipes

After all is said and done, cooking vegetarian recipes should be an easy and exciting adventure. Every recipe in this book is quite simple to make and as tasty as any meat-based alternative, if not more so.

To set yourself up for success, be sure to read any recipe you choose to cook carefully and in its entirety (especially the instructions) so that you completely understand each step. You can always bookmark and refer to the definitions of cooking techniques and essential tools in this chapter. Yields are commonly listed to serve 4, but you can always scale down the amounts of each ingredient to best suit your needs. On the other hand, batch cooking gives you lunch and dinner leftovers.

Every recipe in this book will have at least one of the following labels to help you decide what to cook:

- **DAIRY-FREE:** contains no dairy products

- **SOY-FREE:** contains no soy products

- **NUT-FREE:** is free of nuts

- **GLUTEN-FREE:** is free of gluten

- **VEGAN:** is free of any type of animal product or by-product

- **30-MINUTE MEAL:** can be prepared, cooked, and served in 30 minutes or less

- **5 MAIN INGREDIENTS:** uses only five main ingredients (excluding olive oil, salt, and pepper)

You will also find some useful tips and tricks included alongside the recipes, like how to change up ingredients to achieve a different flavor, and kitchen hacks to make cooking even simpler.

All in all, I hope you are excited to dive into the world of creating vegetarian meals and that you find all of the recipes in this book to be easy, fun, and full of flavor!

BLUEBERRY-BANANA
PROTEIN PANCAKES, PAGE 26

chapter 2
BREAKFAST

Breakfast may be the most important meal of the day, but for busy teens, it may seem difficult to find the time to power up for the day ahead. Fortunately, all of the recipes in this chapter are super easy to put together, even on the busiest of mornings, and some can even be made ahead and stored for a grab-and-go meal.

CHEESY VEGGIE SCRAMBLE

30-MINUTE MEAL, GLUTEN-FREE, NUT-FREE, SOY-FREE
SERVES: 4 • **PREP TIME:** 10 minutes • **COOK TIME:** 10 minutes

INGREDIENTS

8 eggs
¼ teaspoon
    chili powder
Salt and pepper,
    to taste
3 garlic cloves, minced
½ cup diced red
    bell pepper
½ white onion, diced
½ cup chopped
    mushrooms
1 cup grated smoked
    Gouda cheese
Canola oil
2 cups spinach

TOOLS

Cutting board
Handheld grater
Knife (paring)
Measuring cups
    and spoons
Mixing bowl
Nonstick pan
Spatula or
    wooden spoon
Whisk or fork

One of the easiest breakfast recipes you can make that ensures you are getting a healthy dose of nutrients in your day is a veggie-packed scramble. This one has a delicious blend of fresh vegetables, spices, and smoky Gouda cheese. The cheese and spices make it seem like you're not even eating a ton of vegetables, yet this scramble is packed with good-for-you nutrients.

1. In a mixing bowl, beat the eggs, chili powder, salt, and pepper with a whisk or fork until well combined. Set aside.

2. On a cutting board, use a paring knife to mince the garlic, dice the red pepper (see Kitchen Hack on page 42) and onion, and chop the mushrooms. Set aside.

3. Use a handheld grater to grate the Gouda cheese. Set aside.

4. In a nonstick pan over medium heat, heat just enough canola oil to lightly coat the bottom of the pan. Add the garlic, red pepper, onion, and mushrooms to the pan. Sauté for 3 to 4 minutes, or until the onion and garlic start to look translucent.

5. Stir in the spinach using a spatula or wooden spoon, and sauté until the spinach starts to become tender.

6. Add the egg mixture and cheese to the pan and continue cooking, stirring all the ingredients together until the eggs are scrambled and fully cooked.

GARLICKY PAPRIKA EGGS

5 MAIN INGREDIENTS, 30-MINUTE MEAL, NUT-FREE, SOY-FREE
SERVES: 4 • **PREP TIME:** 5 minutes • **COOK TIME:** 15 to 20 minutes

This recipe originates from eastern Europe and is bursting at the seams with flavor. It's also the ultimate protein- and calcium-packed breakfast to support strong bones and athletic performance. The blend of feta cheese, Greek yogurt, paprika, and garlic results in an incredible aroma. When mixed together with over-easy eggs, you've got yourself a serious morning treat.

1 tablespoon butter,
    plus ¼ cup, divided
12 eggs
4 ounces feta cheese
1 cup Greek yogurt
2½ tablespoons
    garlic powder
2½ tablespoons
    paprika

Cutting board
Knife (paring)
Measuring cups
    and spoons
Nonstick pan
Spatula

1. In a nonstick pan over medium heat, melt 1 tablespoon of butter. Add 3 or 4 eggs at a time, depending on how big your pan is, and fry on one side until the whites are mostly solidified, about 3 to 4 minutes. Use a spatula to carefully flip each egg and fry briefly on the other side. Cook longer if you want the yolks to be more solid and less if you like runny eggs. Set the cooked eggs aside. Repeat with the remaining eggs until all 12 are cooked.

2. On a cutting board, use a paring knife to divide the feta cheese into 4 equal portions. Place each portion in a separate serving bowl and top each with ¼ cup of Greek yogurt and 3 cooked eggs.

3. In the same pan, melt the remaining butter. Tilt the pan so that the butter collects on one side and sprinkle the garlic powder and paprika over the butter to make the sauce. Stir it a bit with a spatula, and then pour it on top of the eggs in each bowl. Serve immediately.

SPICY BLACK BEAN VEGGIE BREAKFAST BURRITO

30-MINUTE MEAL, NUT-FREE, SOY-FREE

SERVES: 4 • **PREP TIME:** 5 minutes • **COOK TIME:** 5 minutes

INGREDIENTS

1 tablespoon olive oil
8 eggs
2 teaspoons cumin
Salt and pepper,
    to taste
1 (15-ounce) can
    black beans, rinsed
    and drained
½ cup preshredded
    Monterey
    Jack cheese
4 whole-wheat tortillas
    or sandwich wraps
8 tablespoons
    sour cream
8 tablespoons salsa
    of choice
2 avocados, peeled,
    pitted, and sliced
Hot sauce (optional)

TOOLS

Cutting board
Knife (chef's)
Measuring cups
    and spoons
Medium mixing bowl
Nonstick pan
Spatula or
    wooden spoon
Whisk

Breakfast burritos allow you to blend together your favorite ingredients, like black beans, sour cream, and even your favorite salsa, to start your day with a wonderful mix of Mexican flavors.

1. In a nonstick pan over medium heat, heat the oil.

2. While the oil is heating, whisk together the eggs, cumin, salt, and pepper in a medium mixing bowl. Rinse and drain the beans.

3. Transfer the egg mixture to the pan and cook for about 2 minutes, then add the black beans and Monterey Jack cheese. Using a spatula or wooden spoon, stir until the eggs are scrambled and fully cooked.

4. Lay out the tortillas on plates. Spread 2 tablespoons of sour cream on one half of each tortilla.

5. Divide the scrambled egg mixture evenly among the tortillas and top with salsa.

6. On a cutting board, use a chef's knife to pit, peel, and slice the avocados, and add half of each avocado, plus hot sauce if desired, to each serving.

KITCHEN HACK: To easily prep an avocado, lay it on its side on a cutting board. Hold the avocado in place with one hand on top, and use a chef's knife in the other hand to cut into the side (so the blade is parallel to the cutting board). Slowly rotate the avocado (keeping the knife in place) so that you cut around the full circumference of the pit. Then pull the halves apart, spoon out the pit, and scoop, slice, or dice the avocado flesh however you please.

SUN-DRIED TOMATO & SHALLOT QUICHE

SOY-FREE
SERVES: 4 • **PREP TIME:** 15 minutes • **COOK TIME:** 1 hour 20 minutes

This tasty quiche contains one of my favorite foods: sun-dried tomatoes! Did you know that sun-dried tomatoes have more healthy antioxidants than raw tomatoes? They are full of flavor, and I love the chewy texture. This recipe is a great way to get started using your oven and its baking settings, as you are essentially making a "pie."

INGREDIENTS

Premade frozen
    piecrust
3 garlic cloves, minced
1 shallot, diced
½ cup chopped
    sun-dried tomatoes
1 teaspoon olive oil
4 eggs
1 cup almond milk
Salt and pepper, to taste
½ cup shredded
    cheddar cheese
2 cups arugula

TOOLS

Baking sheet
Cutting board
Fork
Knife (paring)
Measuring cups
    and spoons
Medium mixing bowl
Nonstick pan
Whisk

1. Preheat the oven to 425°F. Make sure there is an oven rack in the middle position.

2. Take the piecrust out of the freezer and let it thaw for about 10 minutes. With a fork, poke small holes in the bottom and sides of the crust. Bake for 15 minutes, then let the crust cool on a rack or on your stovetop.

3. On a cutting board, use a paring knife to mince the garlic, dice the shallot, and chop the sun-dried tomatoes.

4. In a nonstick pan over medium heat, heat the oil and sauté the garlic, shallot, and tomatoes for 5 to 7 minutes. Remove from the heat and set aside.

5. In a medium mixing bowl, whisk together the eggs, almond milk, salt, and pepper.

6. Place the cooled piecrust on a baking sheet, spread the shallot-tomato mixture and the cheese evenly on the bottom of the crust, then spread the arugula evenly over the cheese. Pour the egg mixture on top.

7. Reduce the oven temperature to 350°F and bake for 50 to 55 minutes, until the quiche looks crispy and golden. Let it cool a bit, but serve hot or warm.

KITCHEN HACK: If you want your egg mixture to be a bit thicker, you can add almond flour or whole-wheat flour. Also, if you don't have sun-dried tomatoes on hand, you can use canned or fresh tomatoes as a substitute.

ZESTY AVOCADO TOAST

30-MINUTE MEAL, DAIRY-FREE, NUT-FREE
SERVES: 4 • **PREP TIME:** 15 minutes • **COOK TIME:** 5 minutes

Avocados are one of my favorite sources of omega-3 healthy fats, essential minerals, and vitamins, and they have more potassium than bananas. Plus, they can be used in so many different types of recipes. This recipe has some Latin flavors going on with the cilantro and lime.

4 slices bread
Juice of 1 lime
2 avocados, peeled,
    pitted, and mashed
Salt and pepper,
    to taste
½ red onion, diced
A few fresh
    cilantro sprigs

Cutting board
Fork
Knives (chef's
    and paring)
Small mixing bowl
Spoon

1. Toast each slice of bread until it becomes firm and golden. Avoid overtoasting, as bread can easily end up burnt.

2. On a cutting board, use a chef's knife to halve the lime, and peel and pit the avocado (see Kitchen Hack on page 19). With a spoon, scoop out the flesh of the avocado and transfer it to a small mixing bowl. Use a fork to mash the avocado so that it gets a smoother consistency.

3. Squeeze out as much juice as you can from the lime into the bowl. Mix together using the fork and sprinkle with salt and pepper.

4. On a cutting board, use a paring knife to dice the onion and add it to the mashed avocado.

5. With a spoon, take scoops of the avocado spread and place them on each piece of toast. Spread the avocado concoction evenly and add fresh cilantro, as well as any additional toppings that you desire. Eat immediately!

MIX IT UP: For a little extra flavor, you can add crumbled cheese, red pepper flakes, or chopped scallion on top.

VEGGIE BREAKFAST SANDWICH

30-MINUTE MEAL, NUT-FREE, SOY-FREE
SERVES: 4 • **PREP TIME:** 5 minutes • **COOK TIME:** 10 minutes

INGREDIENTS

2 tomatoes, sliced
2 ounces mozzarella
   cheese, sliced
½ red onion,
   thinly sliced
1 teaspoon olive oil
4 eggs
4 English muffins
2 cups spinach
Fresh basil
Salt and pepper,
   to taste
Balsamic
   vinegar (optional)

TOOLS

Cutting board
Knives (serrated
   and paring)
Measuring cups
   and spoons
Nonstick pan
Small bowl
Spatula
Whisk

Think of this recipe as a caprese salad in breakfast sandwich form. The flavor of basil gives it a refreshing taste, balanced by zingy red onion and the heartiness of eggs. You will barely realize that there is spinach in this breakfast sandwich. Oh, and did I mention it takes only 15 minutes to make?

1. On a cutting board, use a serrated knife to slice the tomatoes. Then use a paring knife to cut the mozzarella into 4 equal slices and slice the red onion.

2. In a nonstick pan over medium heat, heat the oil.

3. While the oil is heating, whisk the eggs in a small bowl until they are well blended. Add the eggs to the pan and cook for 2 minutes on one side. Once the eggs begin firming up, flip with a spatula and cook for another 1 to 2 minutes.

4. Separate the tops and bottoms of the English muffins and heat them up in a toaster so that they are crispy and slightly browned. Set each muffin on a plate.

5. Place ¼ of the eggs on one half of each muffin. Top with a mozzarella cheese slice and a bit of tomato, spinach, red onion, basil, salt, and pepper.

6. Drizzle with balsamic vinegar, if using. Place the other muffin halves on top, and serve.

COCONUT-STRAWBERRY OVERNIGHT OATS

5 MAIN INGREDIENTS, DAIRY-FREE, GLUTEN-FREE, NUT-FREE
SERVES: 4 • **PREP TIME:** 15 minutes, plus overnight to soak

Overnight oats are one of the most popular oatmeal hacks, and for good reason—no cooking on the stove is required. All you do is simply soak oats in your milk of choice overnight. This recipe is slightly sweet, as it calls for berries, honey, and cinnamon. It's almost good enough to have as a dessert!

½ cup chopped
   strawberries
2 cups rolled oats
3 cups coconut milk
2½ tablespoons honey
1 teaspoon cinnamon

Cutting board
Fork or spoon
Knife (paring)
Large glass jar and lid
   or plastic wrap
Measuring cups
   and spoons

1. On a cutting board, use a paring knife to chop the strawberries into small bits.

2. Place them into a large glass jar with the oats, coconut milk, honey, and cinnamon and mix with a fork or spoon until well combined.

3. Using the same fork or spoon, press the mixture down into the jar so that all of the oats are covered in milk (this is how they will fluff up overnight). Cover the jar with its lid or some plastic wrap. Place it in the refrigerator overnight.

4. The next morning, take out the jar, and voilà! Your overnight oats are complete.

KITCHEN HACK: If the oatmeal turns out a bit thick, you can add a little more nut milk to thin the mixture out. If you like your oatmeal warm, you can also heat up the oats the next day in the microwave or in a pan on the stove.

BLUEBERRY-BANANA PROTEIN PANCAKES

5 MAIN INGREDIENTS, 30-MINUTE MEAL, GLUTEN-FREE, SOY-FREE
SERVES: 4 • **PREP TIME:** 10 minutes • **COOK TIME:** 5 minutes

INGREDIENTS

4 bananas, peeled
   and mashed
4 eggs
¼ teaspoon cinnamon
1 scoop protein
   powder (optional)
½ cup blueberries
2 teaspoons
   coconut oil

TOOLS

Cutting board
Fork
Knife (paring)
Measuring cups
   and spoons
Medium mixing bowl
Nonstick pan
Spatula
Spoon

Did you know you can make pancakes without any flour? Yup, that's right. With this technique, we are creating pancakes from just bananas and eggs to create almost exactly the same flavor as traditional, fluffy pancakes.

1. Peel the bananas and, on a cutting board, use a paring knife to slice them up. Transfer the bananas to a medium mixing bowl and mash them with a fork until smooth.

2. Add the eggs, cinnamon, and protein powder (if using) to the bowl and mix until the ingredients are well blended. Then add the blueberries to the batter, folding them gently in with a fork so that they don't get squished.

3. In a nonstick pan over medium heat, heat the coconut oil. Scoop up a bit of the banana batter with a spoon and transfer it to the hot pan. Spread out the batter with a spatula so that it turns into a disc.

4. Leave the batter in the pan until the bottom of each pancake starts to solidify and the center starts to bubble up. Once the edges of the pancake look golden brown, flip it with the spatula and cook on the other side for 2 to 3 minutes.

5. Serve immediately with your choice of fruits, yogurt, peanut butter, or chocolate.

GARLIC-GINGER BREAKFAST CONGEE

DAIRY-FREE, NUT-FREE
SERVES: 4 • **PREP TIME:** 5 minutes • **COOK TIME:** 50 minutes

Congee is an extremely comforting food originating in Asia. It's a warming blend of rice, veggie broth, and spices. You can make congee for any meal of the day, but this one is perfect for a cold morning when you are craving a hearty meal or when you are feeling extra hungry.

INGREDIENTS

1 tablespoon
    sesame oil
1 (¼-inch) piece of
    fresh ginger, peeled
    and diced
3 garlic cloves, minced
1 cup uncooked
    brown rice
10 cups
    vegetable broth
4 scallions, diced
1 medium
    cucumber, sliced
4 cups baby spinach
Optional toppings:
    soy sauce
    (to taste), kimchi,
    over-easy egg

TOOLS

Cutting board
Knives (chef's
    and paring)
Measuring cups
    and spoons
Medium pot
Spoon
Vegetable peeler

1. In a medium pot over medium heat, heat the sesame oil. While the oil is heating up, use a vegetable peeler to peel the ginger. On a cutting board, use a paring knife to dice the ginger and mince the garlic.

2. Add the ginger, garlic, and brown rice to the pot. Cook for 2 to 3 minutes, then pour the broth into the pan. Bring the mixture to a boil. Once it is boiling, turn down the heat so that it simmers.

3. Cover the pot with a lid and simmer the mixture for about 45 minutes, or until you notice that the rice is turning into a creamy porridge. You can check the pot occasionally and stir with a spoon. If the broth starts to evaporate, you can add some water as needed to make your mixture creamy.

4. While the congee simmers, on a cutting board, use a chef's knife to dice the scallions and slice the cucumber.

5. After 45 minutes, add the spinach to the pot and continue cooking until the spinach becomes wilted, about 4 minutes.

6. Remove the pot from the stove and divide the congee among 4 bowls.

7. Top each bowl with scallions and cucumber.

8. If you like, add kimchi and an over-easy egg on top and drizzle with soy sauce. Enjoy!

MIX IT UP: To turn this dish into a delicious sweet treat, you can simply add honey, sugar, or maple syrup to your base. And top it with fruit instead.

SWEET & SALTY GRANOLA CUPS

DAIRY-FREE, SOY-FREE

MAKES: 6 cups (2 to 3 cups per serving) • **PREP TIME:** 15 minutes •
COOK TIME: 25 minutes

These granola cups are so good that they could be eaten for dessert. I love making them because they are super versatile. You can use all sorts of ingredients for the filling. These granola cups are crunchy, nutty, and delicious!

INGREDIENTS

Nonstick
    cooking spray
1¼ cup rolled oats
½ teaspoon
    vanilla extract
¼ cup maple syrup
1 tablespoon
    coconut oil
¼ cup nut butter
    of choice
Pinch salt
Optional fillings:
    chocolate, fruit,
    yogurt

TOOLS

Knife (table)
Measuring cups
    and spoons
Mixing bowl
Muffin tin (with at
    least 6 cups)
Spatula or
    wooden spoon
Small spoon

1. Preheat the oven to 350°F. Grease 6 cups of a muffin tin with cooking spray and set aside.

2. In a mixing bowl, use a spatula or wooden spoon to mix together the rolled oats, vanilla extract, maple syrup, coconut oil, nut butter, and salt.

3. Fill up each muffin cup in the prepared tin with a small amount of the granola mixture. With a small spoon or with your fingers, spread and push down on the granola so that it becomes thin and creates a little crust. Make sure that the granola mixture comes up the sides of each muffin cup, resembling a little bowl.

4. Bake for 20 to 25 minutes. Once you remove the tin from the oven, you may need to use a small spoon to reshape the granola again. Let the cups cool for about 30 minutes.

5. Use a table knife to remove the granola cups from the muffin tin by running the knife around each cup.

6. Add your fillings of choice to each cup and enjoy these sweet little breakfast treats.

CHIA SEED BREAKFAST PUDDING PARFAIT

DAIRY-FREE, GLUTEN-FREE, SOY-FREE
SERVES: 4 • **PREP TIME:** 10 minutes, plus 2 to 3 hours to soak

If you love pudding, you are going to *love* this protein-packed version. Chia seeds are the star of the show here, lending a crunchy, interesting texture to any type of smoothie or parfait recipe. This one tastes just like a sweet peanut butter and jelly sandwich (without the bread), but with healthy and wholesome ingredients.

½ cup chia seeds
1¼ cup nut milk
    of choice
½ teaspoon
    vanilla extract
4 tablespoons honey
1 banana, peeled
    and sliced
4 tablespoons
    peanut butter
4 tablespoons jelly or
    jam of choice

Cutting board
Jars (4)
Knife (paring)
Measuring cups
    and spoons
Mixing bowl
Whisk

1. In a mixing bowl, lightly whisk together the chia seeds and nut milk. Add the vanilla extract and honey, whisking until well blended.

2. Place the bowl in the refrigerator and let the mixture soak for 2 to 3 hours. Make sure all the chia seeds are evenly distributed so that they don't clump together.

3. Just before serving, peel the banana. On a cutting board, use a paring knife to cut it into slices.

4. To serve, transfer a few dollops of the chilled pudding to 4 glass jars, then start creating layers on top with the peanut butter, sliced banana, and jelly. Enjoy!

INGREDIENT TIP: Aren't familiar with chia seeds? These are protein-packed seeds that also contain healthy fats, fiber, and minerals, like zinc and magnesium. They are extremely versatile and can be added to salads, smoothies, and of course, your breakfast parfait recipes.

THE ULTIMATE BREAKFAST SMOOTHIE

5 MAIN INGREDIENTS, 30-MINUTE MEAL, DAIRY-FREE, SOY-FREE
SERVES: 4 • **PREP TIME:** 5 minutes

INGREDIENTS

2 apples, halved and
    cored
1 cup ice
2 bananas
4 tablespoons
    peanut butter
2 tablespoons honey
1 teaspoon cinnamon

TOOLS

Blender
Cutting board
Knife (chef's)
Measuring cups
    and spoons

Smoothies are one of my favorite go-to breakfast recipes because they are fast to make and even easier to prepare. You are simply putting together ingredients in a blender, pressing "start," and waiting for the ingredients to blend for a few minutes, and then you have a healthy treat ready to drink. It's that easy!

1. On a cutting board, use a chef's knife to cut the apples in half and remove the cores.
2. Place the ice, bananas, apple, and peanut butter in a blender, and blend until smooth.
3. Add the honey and cinnamon, and continue to blend until everything is well combined. Drink immediately.

BERRY MEDLEY SMOOTHIE

30-MINUTE MEAL, GLUTEN-FREE, NUT-FREE, SOY-FREE, VEGAN

SERVES: 4 • **PREP TIME:** 10 minutes

I love the tangy flavors of berries and the fact that they are packed with vitamins and antioxidants. This berry smoothie is colorful, vibrant, and deliciously pumped up with protein. A lot of people think you need to have tons of protein powder in a smoothie to get any protein out of it, but adding a bit of Greek yogurt alone gives you a nice dose.

1. Place the bananas, berries, yogurt, and almond milk in a blender, and blend until smooth.
2. Add the spinach, and continue to blend until everything is well combined. Serve immediately.

INGREDIENT TIP: You can barely notice the flavor of spinach when it's added to a smoothie, so it's a good idea to add some whenever making one to sneak some extra nutrients into your diet.

2 bananas
3 cups frozen
   mixed berries
2 cups Greek yogurt
2½ cups almond milk
3 cups fresh spinach

Blender
Measuring cups

GREEN MACHINE SMOOTHIE

30-MINUTE MEAL, DAIRY-FREE, GLUTEN-FREE, NUT-FREE, SOY-FREE

SERVES: 4 • **PREP TIME:** 10 minutes

INGREDIENTS

2 avocados, peeled
and pitted
2 teaspoons
vanilla extract
4 cups coconut milk
2 cups spinach
4 tablespoons honey
or maple syrup

TOOLS

Blender
Cutting board
Knife (chef's)
Measuring cups
and spoons
Spoon

This lean and green smoothie recipe may look like it has tons of veggies in it, but it tastes super creamy and delicious. The avocado and spinach do not create an overpowering flavor at all, and the honey and vanilla extract provide a nice dose of sweetness. You can also add a banana if you want to sweeten it up a bit more.

1. On a cutting board, use a chef's knife to peel and pit the avocados (see Kitchen Hack on page 19). Use a spoon to scoop out the flesh and place it in a blender.

2. Add the vanilla extract, coconut milk, spinach, and honey to the blender, and blend together until well mixed. Serve immediately.

CHEESY JALAPEÑO BISCUITS

GLUTEN-FREE, SOY-FREE

MAKES: 10 biscuits (1 biscuit per serving) • **PREP TIME:** 20 minutes •
COOK TIME: 20 minutes

One of my favorite memories growing up is eating freshly baked cheddar biscuits. These cheesy biscuits are the ideal breakfast to keep you full and satisfied until lunch, plus they are completely grain-free! They are made with gluten-free almond flour (which is simply ground-up almonds), delicious cheeses, and jalapeños (if you want to spice it up).

1. Preheat the oven to 350°F. Use a handheld grater to grate the Gouda cheese while the oven heats up. Set aside.

2. On a cutting board, use a paring knife to mince the garlic and dice the jalapeño, if using. Set aside.

3. Use a handheld mixer or stand mixer to beat together the Gouda cheese, cream cheese, and egg until well combined.

4. Add the minced garlic, onion powder, oregano, and parsley, and continue mixing together in pulses with the mixer.

5. Add the heavy cream, water, and almond flour to the mixture, and mix until everything is well combined.

6. If you are using jalapeños, fold them in with a spatula or wooden spoon.

7. Grease 10 cups of a muffin tin with cooking spray, then spoon generous dollops of biscuit dough into the cups.

8. Bake for about 20 minutes, or until the tops look fluffy, crisp, and slightly golden. Remove and let them cool for about 30 minutes.

2 cups grated smoked Gouda cheese
3 garlic cloves, minced
¼ cup diced jalapeño peppers (optional)
4 ounces cream cheese, softened
1 egg
½ teaspoon onion powder
½ teaspoon oregano
½ teaspoon parsley
¼ cup heavy cream
¼ cup water
1½ cups almond flour
Nonstick cooking spray

Cutting board
Handheld grater
Handheld mixer or stand mixer
Knife (paring)
Measuring cups and spoons
Medium mixing bowl
Muffin tin (with at least 10 cups)
Spatula or wooden spoon

MANDARIN ORANGE
SALAD, PAGE 39

chapter 3
SOUPS & SALADS

Soups and salads are a breeze when you're a vegetarian, and this chapter is packed with recipes that will delight your taste buds while also ensuring you get loads of nutritional value.

SWEET WALNUT APPLE SALAD

30-MINUTE MEAL, GLUTEN-FREE, SOY-FREE

SERVES: 4 • **PREP TIME:** 10 minutes

INGREDIENTS

2 apples, cored
and diced
½ cup raw walnuts,
broken into
smaller pieces
6 cups spinach
½ cup crumbled
feta cheese
1 tablespoon honey
3 tablespoons
balsamic vinegar
¼ cup olive oil

TOOLS

Cutting board
Forks or large
spoons (2)
Knife (chef's)
Large mixing bowl
Measuring cups
and spoons
Small mixing bowl
Whisk

This salad is one of my go-tos, especially during the summer months when I want something light and refreshing. It is an ultra-flavorful salad sprinkled with crunchy walnuts (which are packed with healthy fats and protein), sweet apples, and salty feta.

1. On a cutting board, use a chef's knife to core and dice the apples, then cut the walnuts into smaller pieces.
2. In a large mixing bowl, combine the spinach, apples, walnuts, and feta.
3. In a small mixing bowl, whisk together the honey, balsamic vinegar, and olive oil. Drizzle the dressing on top of the salad in the large bowl.
4. Using 2 forks or large spoons, toss the salad well. Serve immediately.

MIX IT UP: Any type of nut will be a wonderful addition to this salad. If you're not a fan of walnuts, crumbled pecans or slivered almonds also taste great. Regardless which type of nut you choose, you will be adding delicious flavor and crunchy texture.

MANDARIN ORANGE SALAD

DAIRY-FREE, GLUTEN-FREE, SOY-FREE, VEGAN
SERVES: 4 • **PREP TIME:** 10 minutes

This is a fruit-focused salad that I adapted from my mom's recipe, as it was a staple in many of our meals growing up. I love putting fruits in salads because it makes me feel like I'm getting a bit of sweetness in with my healthy meal. This salad is also pumped up with a ton of vitamin C—one of the most important vitamins you can get—from the oranges and the mixed greens.

1. Rinse and drain the mandarin oranges. Set aside.
2. On a cutting board, use a chef's knife to chop the mixed greens, and use a paring knife to chop the red onion.
3. In a large mixing bowl, combine the mandarin oranges, greens, red onion, almonds, olive oil, vinegar, salt, and pepper.
4. Using 2 forks or large spoons, toss the salad well. Serve immediately.

1 (11-ounce) can mandarin oranges in water, rinsed and drained
6 cups mixed greens, chopped
1 red onion, chopped
1 cup slivered almonds
¼ cup olive oil
3 tablespoons red wine vinegar
Salt and pepper, to taste

Cutting board
Forks or large spoons (2)
Knives (chef's and paring)
Large mixing bowl
Measuring cups and spoons

MANGO RICE SALAD

SOY-FREE, VEGAN
SERVES: 4 • **PREP TIME:** 15 minutes • **COOK TIME:** 20 minutes

INGREDIENTS

1 cup uncooked
    multicolored rice
1 mango, peeled,
    pitted, and diced
1 cucumber, sliced
2 scallions, chopped
Juice of 1 orange
3 tablespoons red
    wine vinegar
¼ cup olive oil
4 cups arugula

TOOLS

Cutting board
Forks or large
    spoons (2)
Knife (chef's)
Large mixing bowl
Measuring cups
    and spoons
Medium pot
Small mixing bowl
Vegetable peeler
Whisk

Mangos and rice may seem like an odd combination, but this recipe marries them together in a beautifully flavorful partnership. Full of antioxidants, vitamins, and healthy carbohydrates, this salad has it all. Depending on the season, you can eat this salad while the rice is warm, or you can chill the cooked rice in the refrigerator for a few hours to make it a refreshing cold dish.

1. In a medium pot, cook the rice according to the package directions.
2. While the rice is cooking, on a cutting board, use a vegetable peeler to peel the mango, and use a chef's knife to slice it away from the pit. Dice each of the mango slices, slice the cucumber, chop the scallions, and halve the orange.
3. In a small mixing bowl, squeeze out as much juice as you can from the orange, being careful to catch and discard the seeds. Add the vinegar and olive oil, whisking to combine.
4. In a large mixing bowl, combine the arugula, rice, mango, cucumber, scallions, and dressing, tossing together with 2 forks or large spoons. Serve immediately.

DINO KALE CAESAR SALAD

5 MAIN INGREDIENTS, 30-MINUTE MEAL, NUT-FREE, SOY-FREE
SERVES: 4 • **PREP TIME:** 10 minutes

You cannot have a cookbook without a Caesar salad recipe! When you have Caesar salad dressing on hand, this is one of the easiest ways to whip up a side salad in no time. This recipe is not only creamy, cheesy, and satisfying but also extra healthy since it includes a superfood: kale. If you are new to eating kale, this recipe calls for dinosaur or baby kale (also called lacinato kale). Both varieties are less bitter and have a less chewy texture than regular kale.

Juice of 1 lemon
8 cups dino or
     baby kale
⅔ cup vegetarian
     Caesar salad
     dressing
1 cup croutons

Cutting board
Forks or large
     spoons (2)
Knife (chef's)
Large mixing bowl
Measuring cups

1. On a cutting board, use a chef's knife to halve the lemon. In a large mixing bowl, squeeze out as much juice as you can, being careful to catch and discard the seeds.
2. Add the kale to the bowl, toss it in the lemon juice, and massage it with your hands for about 1 minute. Set it aside for 5 to 7 minutes. This will help enhance the kale's texture and flavor so that it tastes extra delicious.
3. Top the salad with the Caesar salad dressing and croutons. Using 2 forks or large spoons, toss the salad well. Serve immediately.

INGREDIENT TIP: If you don't have croutons on hand, you can preheat the oven to 375°F, sprinkle a piece of bread with garlic, and bake it for about 10 minutes. Voilà! Instant croutons for your salad.

GREEK ISLANDS SALAD

30-MINUTE MEAL, GLUTEN-FREE, NUT-FREE, SOY-FREE
SERVES: 4 • **PREP TIME:** 15 minutes

INGREDIENTS

2 heads romaine
    lettuce, chopped
2 green bell peppers,
    seeded and sliced
1 red onion, sliced
Juice of 1 lemon
¼ cup olive oil
¼ cup red wine vinegar
1 (15-ounce) can
    chickpeas, rinsed
    and drained
¼ cup pickled
    poblano peppers
1 cup pitted
    kalamata olives
½ cup crumbled
    feta cheese

TOOLS

Cutting board
Forks or large
    spoons (2)
Knife (chef's)
Large mixing bowl
Measuring cups
Small mixing bowl
Whisk

This hearty and flavorful salad contains a refreshing blend of chickpeas, lemon, poblano peppers, and a delicious, easy dressing. This combination of vegetables and beans creates a completely well-balanced meal. This recipe offers a twist on a traditional Greek salad, which usually includes cucumbers and tomatoes.

1. On a cutting board, use a chef's knife to chop the romaine lettuce, seed and slice the green peppers (see Kitchen Hack), slice the red onion, and halve the lemon.

2. In a small mixing bowl, squeeze out as much juice as you can from the lemon, being careful to catch and discard the seeds. Add the olive oil and vinegar, whisking to combine. Set aside.

3. Rinse and drain the chickpeas and place them in a large mixing bowl. Add the romaine, green peppers, red onion, poblano peppers, and olives.

4. Pour the dressing over the salad and top with the feta cheese. Using 2 forks or large spoons, toss the salad well. Serve immediately.

KITCHEN HACK: To prepare any type of bell pepper, cut off the top of the pepper with a chef's knife, pull out the core, and scoop out the seeds with your hands before cutting the pepper in half. At that point, you can lay each half flat on the cutting board and slice it into long pieces. You can then chop or dice the pieces further or leave the pieces sliced according to the recipe instructions.

MEXICAN AZTEC SALAD

NUT-FREE, SOY-FREE

SERVES: 4 • **PREP TIME:** 10 minutes

This salad is filled to the brim with flavor and can be eaten as a side salad or even as a main dish. If you do not already have any type of lime or cilantro salad dressing in your fridge, you can create a simple vinaigrette with olive oil, lime juice, and garlic powder. You can also top your salad with cilantro if you like it (usually people either love or hate this herb).

1. On a cutting board, use a chef's knife to shred the romaine lettuce; slice the onion; peel, pit, and dice the avocado (see Kitchen Hack on page 19); and halve the lime.

2. In a small mixing bowl, squeeze out as much juice as you can from the lime. Add the olive oil and garlic powder, whisking to combine. Set aside.

3. Rinse and drain the beans and place them in a large mixing bowl. Add the romaine, onion, avocado, cheese, tomatoes, and black olives. Pour the dressing over the salad, and use 2 forks or large spoons to toss the salad well.

4. Sprinkle with salt and pepper and serve.

1 head romaine lettuce, shredded
1 small red onion, sliced
1 avocado, peeled, pitted, and diced
Juice of 1 lime
¼ cup olive oil
½ teaspoon garlic powder
1 (15-ounce) can red kidney beans, rinsed and drained
1 cup shredded Monterey Jack cheese
1 cup cherry tomatoes
¼ cup canned black olives
Salt and pepper, to taste

Cutting board
Forks or large spoons (2)
Knife (chef's)
Large mixing bowl
Measuring cups and spoons
Small mixing bowl
Whisk

WARM MUSHROOM SPINACH SALAD

GLUTEN-FREE, NUT-FREE, SOY-FREE

SERVES: 4 • **PREP TIME:** 10 minutes • **COOK TIME:** 15 minutes

INGREDIENTS

2 shallots, diced
1 pound brown
   mushrooms,
   chopped
1 tablespoon olive oil,
   plus ¼ cup
2 teaspoons
   garlic powder
6 cups fresh spinach
¼ red wine vinegar
1 cup crumbled
   goat cheese

TOOLS

Cutting board
Forks or large
   spoons (2)
Knives (chef's
   and paring)
Large mixing bowl
Measuring cups
   and spoons
Nonstick pan
Spatula or
   wooden spoon

Sometimes, it is nice to have a warm, comforting salad instead of the chilled version. Spinach is one of my favorite greens to "wilt" for warm salads, and it is one of the best sources of nutrients you can eat. I also love adding mushrooms to my meals during cold winter months, since they can help you prevent colds and fight off illness during flu season.

1. On a cutting board, use a paring knife to dice the shallots. Use a chef's knife to chop the mushrooms. Set both aside.

2. In a nonstick pan over medium heat, heat 1 tablespoon of olive oil. Sauté the shallots for about 4 minutes, or until they start to become translucent.

3. Add the mushrooms and garlic powder, and continue sautéing for about 7 minutes, stirring with a spatula or wooden spoon until the mushrooms become tender.

4. In a large bowl, combine the spinach and sautéed vegetables. Top with the remaining ¼ cup of olive oil and vinegar, and use 2 forks or large spoons to toss the salad well, until the hot veggies start to wilt the spinach. Sprinkle the salad with the goat cheese and serve immediately.

VEGGIE-FORWARD TUSCAN SOUP

GLUTEN-FREE, NUT-FREE, SOY-FREE
SERVES: 4 • **PREP TIME:** 5 minutes • **COOK TIME:** 30 minutes

Give your kitchen a flavorful and aromatic vibe with this soup recipe straight from Tuscany. This ridiculously simple soup is made by tossing all the ingredients into a pot and then leaving it to simmer for just over 30 minutes!

1. On a cutting board, use a vegetable peeler to peel the carrots. Use a chef's knife to chop the carrots, onion, and spinach. Use a paring knife to mince the garlic. Set aside.

2. Rinse and drain the kidney beans and set aside.

3. In a large saucepan over medium-high heat, add a splash of vegetable broth. Sauté the onion, garlic, carrots, and spinach for 7 to 10 minutes, or until the vegetables start to soften.

4. Add the Italian seasoning and continue cooking for 2 to 3 minutes, or until you start to smell the spices.

5. Add the remaining broth, beans, and heavy cream to the saucepan. Give the soup a good stir with a wooden spoon, cover the saucepan with its lid, turn down the heat, and let the soup simmer for 15 minutes.

6. Transfer some soup to a serving bowl. Use a handheld grater to grate some Parmesan cheese over the soup.

DID YOU KNOW? Compared to other vegetables, spinach contains one of the highest levels of antioxidants. These superhero substances help keep your body working in tip-top shape and even protect your skin so that your complexion stays clear and glowing.

3 carrots, peeled
    and chopped
1 large white
    onion, chopped
2 bunches
    spinach, chopped
3 garlic cloves, minced
1 (15-ounce) can white
    kidney beans,
    rinsed and drained
4 cups vegetable
    broth, divided
2 teaspoons
    Italian seasoning
¾ cup heavy cream
Grated vegetarian
    Parmesan cheese
Toasted bread,
    for serving

Cutting board
Handheld grater
Knives (chef's
    and paring)
Large saucepan
Measuring cups
    and spoons
Vegetable peeler
Wooden spoon

SOUPS & SALADS

VEGGIE-PACKED TORTILLA SOUP

30-MINUTE MEAL, GLUTEN-FREE, NUT-FREE, SOY-FREE
SERVES: 4 • **PREP TIME:** 5 minutes • **COOK TIME:** 25 minutes

INGREDIENTS

4 garlic cloves, minced
1 white
    onion, chopped
1 red bell pepper,
    seeded and diced
Juice of 1 lime
6 cups vegetable
    broth, divided
1 (28-ounce) can
    crushed tomatoes
1 (15-ounce) can black
    beans, rinsed
    and drained
1 cup frozen whole-
    kernel corn
1 teaspoon cumin
¼ cup sour cream
Lime wedges, for
    garnish (optional)

TOOLS

Cutting board
Knives (chef's
    and paring)
Measuring cups
    and spoons
Spatula or
    wooden spoon
Stockpot

My go-to appetizer in Mexican restaurants has always been tortilla soup. The creamy combination of cheese, spicy broth, and heartwarming ingredients always leaves me feeling satisfied. I like to whip up this home-made soup whenever the craving strikes! I also like to top my tortilla soup with a big dollop of sour cream to give it an extra-creamy flavor.

1. On a cutting board, use a paring knife to mince the garlic. Use a chef's knife to chop the onion, seed and dice the red pepper (see Kitchen Hack on page 42), and halve the lime. Set aside.

2. In a stockpot over medium heat, add a splash of vegetable broth. Sauté the onion, garlic, and red pepper for 4 to 5 minutes, stirring occasionally with a spatula or wooden spoon, until the onion becomes translucent.

3. Add the remaining broth, tomatoes, black beans, corn, and cumin. Let the soup simmer for about 15 minutes, stirring occasionally.

4. Squeeze the juice from the lime into the pot. Add the sour cream, and stir for another 3 to 4 minutes.

5. If you like, garnish with a lime wedge before serving.

KITCHEN HACK: The lime, cumin, and garlic add flavor to this soup, but if you have adobo seasoning in your pantry, a few sprinkles of this seasoning go a long way, too.

LENTIL SOUP

DAIRY-FREE, GLUTEN-FREE, NUT-FREE, SOY-FREE, VEGAN
SERVES: 4 • **PREP TIME:** 10 minutes • **COOK TIME:** 35 minutes

This is one of the easiest soups you can make, and it is so hearty that it can also be considered a stew. You can heat up or toast a baguette to dip in this soup, or eat it completely by itself. Did you know that lentils are one of the best plant-based sources of protein, too? Once you start to get familiar with cooking lentils, you'll be able to tap into your creativity and add this legume to all sorts of future recipes.

1. On a cutting board, use a vegetable peeler to peel the carrots, then use a chef's knife to chop the carrots and celery. Use a paring knife to mince the garlic and dice the shallots.

2. In a stockpot over medium heat, heat the olive oil and sauté the garlic, shallots, carrots, and celery for about 5 minutes, stirring occasionally with a spatula or wooden spoon.

3. Add the vegetable broth, lentils, paprika, parsley, salt, and pepper. Bring to a boil to cook the lentils.

4. Once the soup is boiling, turn down the heat and simmer for about 25 minutes, or until you notice that the lentils are soft and tender. Taste the soup before serving and adjust the seasonings accordingly. Serve immediately.

4 large carrots, peeled
    and chopped
4 celery
    stalks, chopped
3 garlic cloves, minced
2 shallots, peeled
    and diced
1 tablespoon olive oil
4 cups vegetable broth
1 cup green lentils
1 teaspoon
    smoked paprika
½ teaspoon parsley
Salt and pepper,
    to taste

Cutting board
Knives (chef's
    and paring)
Measuring cups
    and spoons
Spatula or
    wooden spoon
Stockpot
Vegetable peeler

SOUPS & SALADS

MISO BOK CHOY SOUP

NUT-FREE, VEGAN
SERVES: 4 • **PREP TIME:** 10 minutes • **COOK TIME:** 25 minutes

INGREDIENTS

8 ounces firm tofu, drained and cubed
4 heads baby bok choy, chopped
4 scallions, chopped
3 garlic cloves, minced
1 tablespoon sesame oil
½ cup white miso
4 tablespoons soy sauce
4 cups vegetable stock
3 cups water

TOOLS

Cutting board
Knives (chef's and paring)
Measuring cups and spoons
Paper towels
Spatula or wooden spoon
Stockpot

Whenever I'm craving something salty, I always turn to this miso soup recipe. If you are unfamiliar with miso, it is an extremely popular ingredient in Japanese cooking and is super savory and fragrant. It gives recipes a ton of flavor and also contains vitamins and minerals. Miso is even known to help with digestion!

1. Wrap the tofu in a few paper towels and press on it to remove any excess liquid (this helps the tofu infuse with the flavors you use in your cooking). On a cutting board, use a chef's knife to cube the drained tofu and chop the bok choy and scallions. Use a paring knife to mince the garlic. Set the bok choy and scallions aside.

2. In a stockpot over medium heat, heat the sesame oil. Add the garlic, tofu, white miso, and soy sauce, and cook for 3 to 4 minutes, stirring occasionally with a spatula or wooden spoon.

3. Add the vegetable stock, water, and bok choy, and simmer for 15 to 20 minutes. Sprinkle with the scallions and serve.

INGREDIENT TIP: Bok choy is a Chinese cabbage that has a wonderful nutty flavor when it's sautéed or simmered. Baby bok choy is a slightly sweeter and smaller version of regular bok choy. This ingredient can be also be used in stir-fries or roasted recipes.

GREEK LEMON SOUP

NUT-FREE, SOY-FREE

SERVES: 4 • **PREP TIME:** 10 minutes • **COOK TIME:** 35 minutes

The traditional name for this soup is avgolemono, and it typically includes chicken. In this vegetarian recipe, we are keeping all the wonderful flavors but removing the meat. If you love lemons, you will especially love this soup, because the citrus flavor really brings everything together. This soup will make you want to cozy up on the couch in a blanket!

3 garlic cloves, minced
2 carrots, diced
Juice of 2 lemons
2 tablespoons olive oil
4 cups vegetable stock
1 cup uncooked
   brown or white
   jasmine rice
Salt and pepper,
   to taste
4 eggs
Small handful fresh
   dill, chopped

Cutting board
Knives (chef's
   and paring)
Whisk
Measuring cups
   and spoons
Medium mixing bowl
Spatula or
   wooden spoon
Stockpot

1. On a cutting board, use a paring knife to mince the garlic, and use a chef's knife to dice the carrots and halve the lemons. Set the lemons aside.

2. In a stockpot over medium-low heat, heat the olive oil. Sauté the garlic and carrots for about 7 minutes, stirring occasionally with a spatula or wooden spoon.

3. Add the vegetable stock, rice, salt, and pepper, and bring to a boil. Once the soup is boiling, reduce the heat, cover the pot with its lid, and let it simmer for about 10 minutes, or until the rice is tender.

4. In a medium mixing bowl, squeeze out as much juice as you can from the lemons, being careful to catch and discard the seeds. Add the eggs and whisk to combine. Add a cup or two of the soup broth to the egg mixture, stirring as you slowly add the broth.

5. Add the egg mixture back into the soup and continue simmering for about 4 minutes. Top the soup with dill and enjoy!

CHILLED CUCUMBER SOUP

NUT-FREE, SOY-FREE

SERVES: 4 • **PREP TIME:** 15 minutes • **CHILL TIME:** 2 hours or overnight

INGREDIENTS

2 English cucumbers,
    chopped
Juice of 2 lemons
3 garlic cloves, minced
4 fresh dill sprigs
4 cups water
1 teaspoon
    onion powder
3 cups Greek yogurt
¼ cup olive oil

TOOLS

Blender
Cutting board
Knives (chef's
    and paring)
Measuring cups
    and spoons

This soup is almost like a chilled tzatziki. If you're unfamiliar with tzatziki, it's a thick, flavorful sauce made with a blend of dill, Greek yogurt, and cucumber that is used in many Mediterranean recipes. Oh, and did I mention that this soup doesn't require any cooking? Chilled soups are extremely popular in the Mediterranean region since the weather there is typically hot. All you have to do for this recipe is combine all the ingredients in a blender.

1. On a cutting board, use a chef's knife to chop the cucumbers and halve the lemons. Use a paring knife to mince the garlic.

2. In a blender, squeeze out as much juice as you can from the lemons, being careful to catch and discard the seeds. Add the cucumbers, garlic, dill, water, onion powder, yogurt, and olive oil, and blend until smooth.

3. Place the blender jar, covered, in the refrigerator to chill overnight or for at least 2 hours. Serve cold.

KITCHEN HACK: Once you remove the soup from the fridge, you can season with salt and pepper to taste, or you can drizzle more olive oil or lemon juice over it. I love the fact that this soup can be in the fridge overnight, because that really allows time for all of the flavors to combine.

HEARTY CREAM OF TOMATO SOUP

GLUTEN-FREE, NUT-FREE, SOY-FREE
SERVES: 4 • **PREP TIME:** 10 minutes • **COOK TIME:** 25 minutes

You have most likely grown up on tomato soup, but now as a young adult, you can make it a bit healthier. This recipe uses simple ingredients to create lasting flavor, and once the ingredients are prepped, it can be ready in under 30 minutes.

1. On a cutting board, use a chef's knife to chop the white onion, and use a paring knife to mince the garlic.

2. In a stockpot over medium heat, heat the olive oil. Add the onion, garlic, and canned tomatoes, and cook for about 5 minutes.

3. Add the vegetable broth, Italian seasoning, salt, and pepper. Bring to a simmer and cook for about 15 minutes.

4. Add the heavy cream and cook for another 4 minutes.

5. Remove the pot from the stove and let it cool for about 10 minutes before transferring the tomato mixture to a blender and adding the fresh basil.

6. Blend all the ingredients until they reach a smooth consistency. Once the soup is blended well, you can serve and enjoy it!

1 white
    onion, chopped
3 garlic cloves, minced
1 tablespoon olive oil
1 (28-ounce) can
    crushed or
    chopped tomatoes
3 cups vegetable broth
1 teaspoon
    Italian seasoning
Salt and pepper,
    to taste
1 cup heavy cream
1 tablespoon chopped
    fresh basil

Blender
Cutting board
Knives (chef's
    and paring)
Measuring cups
    and spoons
Stockpot

SWEET POTATO
FRIES, PAGE 62

chapter 4
SNACKS & SIDES

Snacks and sides keep life interesting, and this chapter brings you an assortment that will make your taste buds dance. These recipes are also packed with nutrition to help you power through whatever comes next, whether it's getting through a pile of homework, soccer practice, or that science project.

BREADED RICOTTA SPINACH BALLS

NUT-FREE, SOY-FREE

MAKES: About 10 balls (2 balls per serving) • **PREP TIME:** 10 minutes •
COOK TIME: 40 minutes

INGREDIENTS

Nonstick
   cooking spray
1 cup grated
   Gouda cheese
1 (10-ounce) package
   frozen spinach,
   thawed
1 (15-ounce) container
   ricotta cheese
1 teaspoon
   garlic powder
1 teaspoon
   onion powder
2 eggs
1 cup bread crumbs,
   plus 3 tablespoons
1 teaspoon
   Italian seasoning
Salt and pepper,
   to taste

TOOLS

Aluminum foil
Baking sheet
Handheld grater
Large mixing bowl
Measuring cups
   and spoons
Small mixing bowl
Spatula

This cheesy breaded appetizer is a crowd-pleaser that tastes extra delicious when dipped in marinara sauce or ranch dressing. It is so difficult to even tell that there is spinach in it! These breaded ricotta balls are easy to prepare and take only 10 minutes of hands-on work. After you create your breaded mixture, you simply pop them in the oven, watch an episode of your favorite show, and then enjoy your delicious snack.

1. Preheat the oven to 375°F. Line a baking sheet with aluminum foil and spray with cooking spray. Set aside.

2. Use a handheld grater to grate the Gouda cheese into a large mixing bowl.

3. Thaw the spinach in the microwave according to the package directions and add it to the same bowl. Use a spatula to stir in the ricotta, garlic powder, onion powder, eggs, 1 cup of bread crumbs, Italian seasoning, salt, and pepper until well combined.

4. Roll tablespoon-size scoops of the mixture into balls, trying not to make the balls too loose or too tight.

5. Add the remaining 3 tablespoons of bread crumbs to a small mixing bowl and roll each ball in them to create a crispy exterior.

6. Arrange the balls on the prepared baking sheet and bake for 40 minutes, flipping each ball over at the 20-minute mark. Let them cool before serving.

MIX IT UP: If you like spicy foods, mix equal parts marinara sauce and sour cream, plus a dash of red pepper flakes, to create a creamy and spicy accompaniment to the crunchy texture of the spinach balls.

GUACAMOLE

30-MINUTE MEAL, GLUTEN-FREE, NUT-FREE, SOY-FREE
SERVES: 4 • **PREP TIME:** 15 minutes

INGREDIENTS

Juice of 1 lime
3 avocados, peeled
    and pitted
1 white onion, diced
2 plum
    tomatoes, diced
Minced fresh cilantro,
    for garnish
1 teaspoon
    garlic powder
Salt and pepper,
    to taste
1 tablespoon
    sour cream

TOOLS

Cutting board
Knives (chef's, paring,
    and serrated)
Measuring spoons
Medium mixing bowl
Spoon
Fork

Once you know how to make guacamole, you will be the life of the party no matter where you go. Guacamole is such a popular appetizer for gatherings of friends and family, and for good reason! It is refreshing, flavorful, and goes well with almost any other dish. You can also be creative with your choice of guacamole toppings once you get the hang of making this standard version.

1. On a cutting board, use a chef's knife to halve the lime, and peel and pit the avocados (see Kitchen Hack on page 19), then use a spoon to scoop out the avocado flesh. Use a chef's knife to dice the onions, and use a serrated knife to dice the tomatoes. Use a paring knife to mince the cilantro and set aside.

2. In a medium mixing bowl, squeeze out as much juice as you can from the lime. Add the avocado flesh to the bowl and mash with a fork.

3. Add the onion, tomatoes, garlic powder, salt, and pepper to the bowl, mixing well to combine.

4. Transfer to a serving dish and top with the cilantro and sour cream.

5. If you want to serve the guacamole chilled, cover it with plastic wrap, making sure there are no air bubbles between the wrap and the guacamole so it doesn't brown. Let it chill in the refrigerator for about 30 minutes. This will also help all the flavors infuse together.

CHOCOLATE CHIP TRAIL MIX

5 MAIN INGREDIENTS, GLUTEN-FREE

MAKES: 3½ cups (¼ cup per serving) • **PREP TIME:** 10 minutes

Trail mix is one of my favorite snacks to have on hand whenever I'm on the go. It is a scrumptious blend of sweet and salty, and is packed with healthy fats and nutrients! The combination of cashews and peanuts with sweet, dried fruit and chocolate chips makes this snack recipe almost like a healthy dessert.

1. Combine the cashews and peanuts, dried banana, dried pineapple, chocolate chips, and salt in a large mixing bowl, and shake the bowl until all the ingredients are mixed well.
2. Transfer the trail mix to a large mason jar or resealable plastic bag for storage. The mix will keep for up to a month.

MIX IT UP: Trail mix is very easy to customize, and it's yet another recipe that you can be creative with! Experiment with different ingredients, such as sunflower seeds, pumpkin seeds, raisins, dried cranberries, almonds, walnuts, or whatever you can find in the pantry.

1½ cups mixed cashews
     and peanuts
½ cup dried banana
½ cup dried pineapple
1 cup dark
     chocolate chips
Pinch salt

Large mixing bowl
Mason jar or resealable
     plastic bag
Measuring cups

COCONUT PROTEIN ENERGY BALLS

DAIRY-FREE, SOY-FREE
MAKES: 10 balls (2 balls per serving) • **PREP TIME:** 15 minutes •
CHILL TIME: 1 hour

Another super-simple snack when you're on the move, these coconut protein energy balls are packed with plant-based protein and fiber that will help keep you full in between meals (because no one likes being hangry). Best of all, this recipe does not require any baking or cooking. And if you make enough, you will have a stash to last you all week long!

INGREDIENTS

½ cup rolled oats
¼ cup honey
2 tablespoons preshredded coconut
1 tablespoon chia seeds
1 teaspoon vanilla extract
½ cup creamy peanut butter

TOOLS

Baking sheet
Large mixing bowl
Measuring cups and spoons
Spatula
Spoon

1. In a large mixing bowl, use a spatula to stir together the oats, honey, coconut, chia seeds, vanilla extract, and peanut butter until well combined. This may take 5 or more minutes.

2. Use a spoon to scoop out the dough, and roll the scoops into balls.

3. Arrange the balls on a baking sheet and chill in the refrigerator for 1 hour before serving.

INGREDIENT TIP: If you are not a fan of coconut, you can leave it out and use a scoop of your favorite protein powder instead. You can also use almond butter or cashew butter instead of peanut butter to mix it up.

LOADED CHEDDAR POTATOES

GLUTEN-FREE, NUT-FREE, SOY-FREE
SERVES: 4 • **PREP TIME:** 10 minutes • **COOK TIME:** 30 minutes

The mix of cheese, garlic, and chili powder gives this recipe a burst of savory flavor, and it is an appetizer that can even double as your very own entrée. These loaded cheddar potatoes are extremely rich and packed with nutrients, to boot.

1. Preheat the oven to 425°F. Line a baking sheet with aluminum foil and set aside.

2. Poke holes in the potatoes with a fork. Place them on a microwave-safe plate and cook them in the microwave for 5 minutes. Flip the potatoes over on the plate and microwave for another 4 to 5 minutes.

3. On a cutting board, use a chef's knife to cut each of the potatoes into 4 wedges. Use a spoon to scoop out the flesh from each wedge and set the flesh aside.

4. Arrange the potato skins on the prepared baking sheet and drizzle with 1 tablespoon of olive oil. Bake for about 10 minutes, or until the potatoes are crispy.

5. While the potato skins are baking, on a cutting board, use a chef's knife to seed and chop the bell pepper (see Kitchen Hack on page 42) and dice the scallions. Use a paring knife to mince the garlic. Rinse and drain the black beans and set aside.

6. In a nonstick pan over medium heat, heat the remaining tablespoon of olive oil. Sauté the bell pepper, garlic, salt, and pepper for about

(CONTINUED)

4 medium
    russet potatoes
2 tablespoons olive
    oil, divided
1 bell pepper, seeded
    and chopped
½ cup diced scallions
3 garlic cloves, minced
1 cup canned black
    beans, rinsed
    and drained
Salt and pepper
½ cup cheddar cheese
½ teaspoon
    chili powder

Aluminum foil
Cutting board
Baking sheet
Fork
Knives (chef's
    and paring)
Measuring cups
    and spoons
Microwave-safe plate
Nonstick pan
Small mixing bowl
Spoon

SNACKS & SIDES

5 minutes. Add the scooped-out potato flesh and black beans and cook for another 5 minutes.

7. Take the potato skins out of the oven and add some of the filling to each. Top with the cheese and chili powder. Place the potatoes back in the oven for about 5 minutes, until the cheese is melted.

8. Transfer the potatoes to a serving plate and top with the scallions.

RECIPE NOTE: You can also use your own intuition when it comes to additional toppings for your loaded potatoes. I love adding sour cream on top of my potatoes, as well as pickled jalapeños, diced tomatoes, Greek yogurt, or Guacamole (page 56).

BUFFALO DIP

30-MINUTE MEAL, GLUTEN-FREE, NUT-FREE, SOY-FREE
MAKES: 7 cups (½ cup per serving) • **PREP TIME:** 10 minutes •
COOK TIME: 20 minutes

This is an all-time football season favorite of mine, as we make it for game day, and it is always a huge hit with guests. There are a few secret ingredients that make this dip recipe a healthier alternative to Buffalo chicken dip—cauliflower rice and Greek yogurt. You won't even be able to tell that there is cauliflower in this flavorful dip. The only extra things you'll need are some celery sticks, carrot sticks, or tortilla chips for dipping!

1. Preheat the oven to 450°F. Line a baking dish with parchment paper and set aside.

2. In a large mixing bowl, add the cauliflower rice, Greek yogurt, 1 cup of cheddar, garlic powder, cream cheese, Buffalo wing sauce, olive oil, salt, and pepper. Use a handheld mixer to blend all the ingredients until smooth.

3. Transfer the mixture to the prepared baking dish and top with the remaining cup of cheddar cheese. Bake for about 25 minutes, or until the top looks golden brown.

4. While the dip is baking, on a cutting board, use a chef's knife to chop the scallions.

5. Remove the baking dish from the oven and top the dip with the scallions. Wait until the dip has cooled before serving it.

1 (12-ounce) bag cauliflower rice
1 cup Greek yogurt
2 cups shredded cheddar cheese, divided
2 teaspoons garlic powder
4 ounces cream cheese, softened
1 cup Buffalo wing sauce
1 tablespoon olive oil
Salt and pepper, to taste
Chopped scallions, for garnish

Baking dish
Cutting board
Handheld mixer
Knife (chef's)
Large mixing bowl
Parchment paper

SWEET POTATO FRIES

DAIRY-FREE, GLUTEN-FREE, NUT-FREE, SOY-FREE, VEGAN
SERVES: 4 • **PREP TIME:** 10 minutes • **COOK TIME:** 35 minutes

INGREDIENTS

Nonstick
      cooking spray
2 large sweet potatoes,
      sliced
3 tablespoons
      coconut oil
2 tablespoons
      cornstarch
½ teaspoon
      garlic powder
½ teaspoon
      chili powder
½ teaspoon paprika
Salt and pepper,
      to taste

TOOLS

Aluminum foil
Baking sheet
Cutting board
Knife (chef's)
Large mixing bowl
Measuring spoons
Spatula

My personal favorite type of fries is sweet potato fries because I know I am satisfying my craving while getting healthy nutrients into my system. These come with a salty, slightly spicy kick and will hopefully become one of your favorite snacks, too. They can be dipped in ranch dressing, aioli sauce, or plain ketchup—just like regular fries!

1. Preheat the oven to 425°F. Line a baking sheet with aluminum foil, spray with cooking spray, and set aside.

2. On a cutting board, use a chef's knife to slice the sweet potatoes into long, thin wedges or sticks (peeling the skin off is optional).

3. In a large mixing bowl, toss the sweet potatoes with the coconut oil and cornstarch until the fries are coated. Add the garlic powder, chili powder, paprika, salt, and pepper and toss again with your hands.

4. Place the fries in a single layer on the prepared baking sheet, making sure they are spaced out evenly. If there is not enough room on the baking sheet for one layer of fries, you can make a second batch.

5. Bake for about 25 minutes, flipping the fries over halfway through the cooking time with a spatula. Once done, remove the fries and let them cool for a few minutes before serving.

BAKED PEPPER POPPERS

30-MINUTE MEAL, GLUTEN-FREE, NUT-FREE, SOY-FREE
SERVES: 4 • **PREP TIME:** 15 minutes • **COOK TIME:** 15 minutes

If you like jalapeños, you will fall in love with these spicy, cheesy peppers. A lot of pepper poppers are fried, but I choose to bake them to make them a little healthier. These are ready in 30 minutes flat and are easy to assemble.

1. Preheat the oven to 400°F. Line a baking sheet with parchment paper and set aside.

2. On a cutting board, use a paring knife to mince the garlic and chives, and cut the jalapeños in half lengthwise. Use a spoon to remove the seeds and insides from the jalapeños.

3. In a medium mixing bowl, use a spatula or wooden spoon to mix together the cream cheese, garlic, cheddar cheese, cumin, onion powder, salt, and pepper.

4. Arrange the jalapeño peppers on the baking sheet cut-side up, and fill each with the cream cheese mixture.

5. Bake for about 15 minutes, or until you notice the peppers are becoming tender and wilted. Let them cool slightly before serving.

KITCHEN HACK: When cooking with jalapeños, make sure that you wash your hands thoroughly after cutting or handling any jalapeño seeds. Because they are so spicy, the residue from the seeds can linger on your skin and cause a burning sensation if you then touch your nose or eyes.

3 garlic cloves, minced
2 tablespoons minced fresh chives
8 jalapeño peppers, halved and seeded
8 ounces cream cheese, softened
½ cup shredded white cheddar cheese
1 teaspoon cumin
1 teaspoon onion powder
Salt and pepper, to taste

Baking sheet
Cutting board
Knife (paring)
Medium mixing bowl
Parchment paper
Spatula or wooden spoon
Spoon

SNACKS & SIDES

EGGPLANT RICOTTA CHEESE ROLL-UPS

GLUTEN-FREE, NUT-FREE, SOY-FREE
SERVES: 4 • **PREP TIME:** 20 minutes • **COOK TIME:** 40 minutes

This is another recipe that I sometimes catch myself eating as an entrée. It is that good! This Italian dish includes creamy ricotta cheese, refreshing basil, and a blend of Italian seasoning, garlic, and olive oil to create a rich flavor. These are great to make when you are having friends or family over, since the presentation is pretty impressive, too!

INGREDIENTS

2 medium
   eggplants, sliced
3 garlic cloves, minced
¼ cup chopped
   fresh basil
Olive oil, for greasing,
   plus ¼ cup
Salt and pepper,
   to taste
1 (10-ounce) container
   ricotta cheese
1 cup shredded
   mozzarella cheese
1 teaspoon
   onion powder
3 teaspoons Italian
   seasoning, divided
1 cup marinara sauce

TOOLS

Baking dish
Baking sheet
Cutting board
Fork
Handheld mixer
Knives (chef's
   and paring)
Measuring cups
   and spoons
Medium mixing bowl
Paper towel
Parchment paper
Spoon

1. Preheat the oven to 400°F. Line a baking sheet with parchment paper and grease a baking dish with olive oil. Set aside.

2. On a cutting board, use a chef's knife to cut the ends off of each eggplant, then slice the eggplants into ¼-inch-thick slices. Use a paring knife to mince the garlic and chop the basil.

3. Arrange the eggplant slices on the prepared baking sheet and sprinkle salt on both sides. Let them sit for about 15 minutes to soak in the salt, or until beads of liquid form on the surface and the vegetable starts to look a little shriveled. The salt removes excess moisture that can create a bitter taste. Pat the slices dry with a paper towel.

4. Drizzle the eggplant slices with the remaining olive oil and bake for 10 minutes.

5. Meanwhile, in a medium mixing bowl, use a handheld mixer to mix together the ricotta cheese, mozzarella cheese, basil, garlic, onion powder, and 2 teaspoons of Italian seasoning.

6. Remove the eggplant slices from the oven, and spoon a few scoops of the mixture onto each slice. Roll each slice up with a fork (so you don't burn yourself) and place the roll-ups side by side in the prepared baking dish.

7. Pour the marinara sauce over the roll-ups and top them with the basil and the remaining 1 teaspoon of Italian seasoning.

8. Bake the roll-ups for 25 to 30 minutes, or until you see that the marinara sauce is bubbling. Let them cool before serving.

DID YOU KNOW? Not all cheese is vegetarian. Cheeses like Parmesan, Gorgonzola, Pecorino Romano, and Gruyère have to be made with what is called animal rennet, which is not vegetarian. Many other cheeses, like the ones in this cookbook, can be found with vegetarian rennet, making it important to always check the labels on your cheese. Look for "vegetable rennet" or "microbial rennet."

CAULIFLOWER MASHED POTATOES

30-MINUTE MEAL, GLUTEN-FREE, NUT-FREE, SOY-FREE
SERVES: 4 • **PREP TIME:** 5 minutes • **COOK TIME:** 15 minutes

INGREDIENTS

1 head cauliflower,
    chopped
1 tablespoon chopped
    fresh chives
3 garlic cloves, peeled
½ cup shredded
    sharp white
    cheddar cheese
Salt and pepper,
    to taste
3 tablespoons
    butter, divided
4 tablespoons
    sour cream

TOOLS

Blender
Cutting board
Knife (chef's)
Measuring cups
    and spoons
Saucepan with
    steamer insert

Mashed potatoes are among the most common comfort foods, but sometimes recipes call for a lot of butter and cream, making them unhealthy. With this recipe, you can have as much as you want, without the guilt! Integrating cauliflower into this dish transforms it into a superfood powerhouse. Try this recipe with mushroom gravy, lentil meatloaf, or any type of savory main dish.

1. On a cutting board, use a chef's knife to cut the stem off the cauliflower, chop the cauliflower into florets, and chop the chives. Peel the garlic cloves.

2. Place a steamer insert inside of a saucepan. Fill the bottom of the saucepan with water. The water should not reach the bottom of the steamer insert.

3. Add the cauliflower and garlic to the steamer insert, then bring the water to a boil. Cover the saucepan with its lid, and steam the cauliflower for about 15 minutes, or until it becomes tender.

4. Transfer the cauliflower and garlic to a blender. Add the cheddar cheese, salt, pepper, butter, and sour cream. Blend all the ingredients together until smooth.

5. Transfer the mixture to a serving bowl, top with the chives, and serve it while hot.

INGREDIENT TIP: Cauliflower can be used as a substitute in many recipes that call for bread, grains, or starches—including pizza bases!

ORANGE GINGER BROCCOLI

30-MINUTE MEAL, DAIRY-FREE, NUT-FREE
SERVES: 4 • **PREP TIME:** 10 minutes • **COOK TIME:** 15 minutes

I love making this orange ginger broccoli when I find myself feeling nostalgic for orange chicken. The flavor profile is extremely similar to the original dish, but with a vegetarian-friendly twist. To make this an easy meal, you can cook a cup of rice as a base and bake a bit of tofu and tempeh, and you'll have a complete meal of protein, grains, and vegetables!

1 (½-inch) piece ginger, peeled and minced
3 garlic cloves, minced
4 cups chopped broccoli
Juice of 2 oranges
1 tablespoon sesame oil
2 tablespoons cornstarch
2 tablespoons water
½ tablespoon honey
1 tablespoon soy sauce
¼ cup rice vinegar

Cutting board
Knives (chef's and paring)
Measuring cups and spoons
Nonstick pan
Small mixing bowl
Spatula or wooden spoon
Whisk

1. On a cutting board, use a paring knife to peel the ginger, then mince the ginger and garlic. Use a chef's knife to chop the broccoli and halve the oranges.

2. In a nonstick pan over medium heat, heat the sesame oil. Sauté the ginger and garlic for 3 minutes.

3. Add the broccoli to the pan and continue sautéing, stirring occasionally with a spatula or wooden spoon, for another 7 minutes.

4. In a small mixing bowl, whisk together the cornstarch and water. Add the honey, soy sauce, and rice vinegar, whisking to blend. Add the mixture to the pan.

5. Squeeze out as much juice as you can from the oranges into the pan, being careful to catch and discard the seeds. Continue cooking for another 5 to 7 minutes. Transfer to a serving bowl and enjoy!

CHEESY PARSNIP GRATIN

SOY-FREE

SERVES: 4 • **PREP TIME:** 10 minutes • **COOK TIME:** 40 minutes

This is a beautiful side dish that I love to make during the holidays since it is so rich and comforting. The blend of cream cheese and cheddar cheese creates a smooth yet sharp flavor, and the flour helps thicken up the sauce, which is made with nut milk. Thyme and shallots give this recipe an earthy flavor. It is so good, you will definitely be scooping up a second serving for yourself!

INGREDIENTS

1 pound parsnips,
    peeled and sliced
2 large potatoes,
    peeled and sliced
2 shallots, sliced
3 garlic cloves, minced
1 tablespoon butter
½ cup almond milk
1 cup cream cheese
2 cups shredded
    cheddar cheese
2 teaspoons thyme
1 tablespoon flour
Salt, to taste

TOOLS

Baking dish
Cutting board
Knives (chef's
    and paring)
Measuring cups
    and spoons
Parchment paper
Saucepan
Spatula or
    wooden spoon
Vegetable peeler

1. Preheat the oven to 400°F. Line a baking sheet with parchment paper and set aside.

2. On a cutting board, use a vegetable peeler to peel the parsnips and potatoes, then use a chef's knife to slice them into thin discs. Use a paring knife to slice the shallots and mince the garlic.

3. Place the parsnip and potato slices in the prepared baking dish.

4. In a saucepan over medium heat, heat the butter and sauté the garlic and shallots for 3 minutes. Then add the almond milk, cream cheese, cheddar cheese, thyme, flour, and salt. Use a spatula or wooden spoon to stir the ingredients together until you get a thick, creamy cheese sauce.

5. Pour the cheese sauce over the parsnips and potatoes, making sure the sauce gets into every corner of the baking dish.

6. Bake for 30 minutes, or until the top starts to bubble and brown. Let it cool before serving it.

CREAMED SPINACH

GLUTEN-FREE, NUT-FREE, SOY-FREE
SERVES: 4 • **PREP TIME:** 10 minutes • **COOK TIME:** 25 minutes

This creamy and decadent creamed spinach recipe will definitely make you feel indulgent. It is a dish your taste buds will absolutely love, as the spinach is bathed in a thick, cheesy sauce. The nutmeg gives it a nice warming flavor. This is a very easy recipe to make as a side dish for a weeknight meal. It creates a dynamic duo with Cauliflower Mashed Potatoes (page 66) or Eggplant Ricotta Cheese Roll-Ups (page 64).

1 (16-ounce) package frozen spinach, thawed
1 medium onion, diced
3 garlic cloves, minced
1 tablespoon olive oil
½ teaspoon nutmeg
¼ cup heavy cream
4 ounces cream cheese
1 cup shredded mozzarella cheese
1 cup shredded provolone cheese
Salt and pepper, to taste

Cutting board
Knives (chef's and paring)
Measuring cups and spoons
Medium saucepan
Wooden spoon

1. Thaw the frozen spinach in the microwave according to the package directions. Set aside.
2. On a cutting board, use a chef's knife to dice the onion, and use a paring knife to mince the garlic.
3. In a medium saucepan over medium heat, heat the olive oil and sauté the onion and garlic for 3 minutes, stirring with a wooden spoon.
4. Add the thawed spinach and continue cooking for about 5 more minutes. Add the nutmeg, heavy cream, cream cheese, mozzarella, and provolone.
5. Cook until all the cheese has melted. Season with salt and pepper before serving.

KIDNEY BEAN SALAD

30-MINUTE MEAL, GLUTEN-FREE, NUT-FREE, SOY-FREE
SERVES: 4 • **PREP TIME:** 15 minutes

This is the ideal salad for a picnic in the park or a family summer barbecue. Bean salad is a superfast recipe to toss together when you are in a pinch, and you will most likely always have the needed ingredients on hand in your pantry. This salad is bursting with salty, tangy, and rich flavors to give you the ultimate salad side dish. Plus, it can be easily doubled if you are entertaining for a bigger group!

INGREDIENTS

1 red onion, chopped
2 celery stalks, diced
2 dill pickles, diced
2 (15-ounce) cans
    kidney beans,
    rinsed and drained
¼ cup mayonnaise
1 teaspoon mustard
1 tablespoon red
    wine vinegar

TOOLS

Cutting board
Knife (paring)
Measuring cups
    and spoons
Large mixing bowl
Spoon

1. On a cutting board, use a paring knife to chop the onion and dice the celery stalks and dill pickles.

2. Rinse and drain the kidney beans and place them in a large mixing bowl. Add the celery, pickles, and onion, tossing gently to combine.

3. Add the mayonnaise, mustard, and vinegar, mixing with a spoon until well combined.

MIX IT UP: Red kidney beans are one of my favorite beans to use in salads, as they are a bit more tender than other beans. However, you can use other beans if you don't have red kidney beans on hand. This recipe would also go well with black beans or white butter beans. You really cannot go wrong when you have ingredients like mayo and mustard in the mix!

LEMONY KALE & FETA SAUTÉ

30-MINUTE MEAL, GLUTEN-FREE, NUT-FREE, SOY-FREE
SERVES: 4 • **PREP TIME:** 5 minutes • **COOK TIME:** 15 minutes

I used to make this side dish almost nightly when I lived in Greece. I picked up a cooking tip or two from my time there, too! One thing I learned is that olive oil and lemons make almost anything taste fantastic, and this is especially true for recipes that call for leafy greens. When eaten raw, kale can be a bit bitter, but when it is cooked with feta, lemons, and olive oil, it is transformed into a mouthwatering treat.

3 garlic cloves, minced
1 shallot, diced
2 medium bunches
    kale, chopped
Juice of 2 lemons
2 teaspoons
    coconut oil
¼ cup water
4 ounces feta cheese
Salt and pepper,
    to taste
4 tablespoons olive oil

Cutting board
Knives (chef's
    and paring)
Measuring cups
    and spoons
Nonstick pan
Wooden spoon

1. On a cutting board, use a paring knife to mince the garlic and dice the shallot. Use a chef's knife to chop the kale and halve the lemons.

2. In a nonstick pan over medium heat, heat the coconut oil and sauté the garlic and shallot for 3 minutes.

3. Add the kale and water to the pan, and continue cooking for about 10 minutes, stirring occasionally with a wooden spoon, until the water starts to evaporate and the kale starts to become tender.

4. Squeeze out as much juice as you can from the lemons into the pan, being careful to catch and discard the seeds. Add the feta, salt, and pepper, and continue cooking until the feta starts to soften and melt into the kale.

5. Transfer to a serving plate, drizzle with the olive oil, and serve warm.

SOBA VEGGIE PEANUT
NOODLE BOWL, PAGE 75

chapter 5
MAINS FOR ONE

If you're the only vegetarian in your family, you'll find yourself needing to cook for one. While it may initially seem like a hassle, this is really a blessing in disguise, as cooking for one will become a great skill to have once you leave home and live on your own.

AVOCADO CHICKPEA PASTA BOWL

30-MINUTE MEAL, NUT-FREE, SOY-FREE
SERVES: 1 • **PREP TIME:** 10 minutes • **COOK TIME:** 10 minutes

INGREDIENTS

½ (16-ounce) pack-
    age uncooked
    macaroni pasta
Juice of 1 lemon
½ red bell
    pepper, diced
¼ red onion, diced
½ avocado, peeled,
    pitted, and diced
¼ (15-ounce) can
    chickpeas, rinsed
    and drained
¼ cup crumbled
    feta cheese
2 tablespoons olive oil
1 teaspoon
    garlic powder
¼ cup fresh
    basil leaves

TOOLS

Colander
Cutting board
Knife (chef's)
Large mixing bowl
Measuring cups
    and spoons
Medium saucepan
Tongs

This avocado chickpea pasta bowl is bursting with salty flavor from the feta cheese and filled with creamy avocado and aromatic basil. This recipe can also be served as a side dish and can be easily scaled for parties as a popular vegetarian entrée. If you want to include even more nutrients and vegetables, you can add diced cucumber, tomato, and even wilted spinach.

1. In a medium saucepan, cook the pasta according to the package directions.

2. While the pasta cooks, on a cutting board, use a chef's knife to halve the lemon, dice the red pepper (see Kitchen Hack on page 42) and red onion, and peel, pit, and dice the avocado (see Kitchen Hack on page 19).

3. Drain the cooked pasta in a colander and place it in a large mixing bowl.

4. Rinse and drain the chickpeas and add them to the mixing bowl. Add the red pepper, avocado, red onion, and feta cheese, and use tongs to mix everything together.

5. Squeeze out as much juice as you can from the lemon into the bowl, being careful to catch and discard the seeds. Add the olive oil, garlic powder, and basil leaves, and toss everything together again until all the ingredients are combined.

6. Chill for 30 minutes in the refrigerator before serving.

SOBA VEGGIE PEANUT NOODLE BOWL

30-MINUTE MEAL, DAIRY-FREE, VEGAN

SERVES: 1 • **PREP TIME:** 15 minutes • **COOK TIME:** 5 minutes

A blend of protein-packed tofu, nutty peanut butter, crisp sliced vegetables, and salty flavorings gives this soba noodle bowl a ton of savory taste. Every time I make this, my mouth waters throughout the whole process. Soba noodles, which are made of buckwheat, are the antioxidant- and protein-rich highlight of this meal.

1. In a medium saucepan, cook the soba noodles according to the package directions.

2. While the noodles are cooking, wrap the tofu in a few paper towels and press on it to remove any excess liquid (this helps the tofu infuse with the flavors you use in your cooking). On a cutting board, use a chef's knife to cube the drained tofu, chop the cabbage, and dice the scallions. Set the cabbage and scallions aside.

3. Drain the cooked noodles in a colander and place them in a large mixing bowl. Set aside.

4. In the same medium saucepan over medium heat, add the sesame oil, peanut butter, rice vinegar, soy sauce, garlic powder, and sugar, stirring with a wooden spoon to combine. You can taste the sauce to see if you need to add more of a specific ingredient.

½ (8-ounce) package
    soba noodles
¾ cup tofu, drained
    and cubed
½ cup chopped
    purple cabbage
2 scallions, diced
1 teaspoon sesame oil
2 tablespoons
    peanut butter
2 tablespoons
    rice vinegar
½ tablespoon
    soy sauce
1 teaspoon
    garlic powder
½ teaspoon sugar

Colander
Cutting board
Knife (chef's)
Large mixing bowl
Measuring cups
    and spoons
Medium saucepan
Paper towels
Wooden spoon

(CONTINUED)

Soba Veggie Peanut Noodle Bowl CONTINUED

5. Add the tofu to the pan and cook for 5 to 7 minutes.

6. Pour the tofu and sauce into the mixing bowl containing the noodles. Add the cabbage and scallions. Mix all the ingredients together, and serve.

MIX IT UP: Not a fan of cabbage? You can always throw in sliced red bell peppers or carrots instead. Any type of vegetable, from edamame to broccoli, can be used in this recipe, as the flavorful sauce will create a delicious coating.

CHIMICHURRI BEAN BOWL

30-MINUTE MEAL, DAIRY-FREE, SOY-FREE, VEGAN
SERVES: 1 • **PREP TIME:** 10 minutes • **COOK TIME:** 10 minutes

Chimichurri is one of my favorite sauces to make. Originating in Argentinian cuisine, it is very garlic forward and uses fresh parsley for an herbaceous taste. It is a very common sauce on steak but also gives incredible flavor to veggie dishes! In this bean bowl, it really brings together all of the ingredients to create an amazing flavor profile.

1. In a medium saucepan, cook the brown rice according to the package directions.
2. While the rice cooks, rinse and drain the black beans and corn, and place them in a medium mixing bowl.
3. On a cutting board, use a chef's knife to dice the red peppers and halve the lemon. Set the red peppers aside. Squeeze out as much juice as you can from the lemon into the mixing bowl, being careful to catch and discard the seeds.
4. Once the rice is done, transfer it to the mixing bowl. Add the olive oil, garlic powder, red peppers, and parsley, using a spatula to mix everything together.
5. Season with salt and pepper, and serve!

1 cup uncooked
    brown rice
½ cup canned black
    beans, rinsed
    and drained
4 tablespoons canned
    corn, rinsed
    and drained
¼ cup jarred roasted
    red peppers, diced
Juice of 1 lemon
4 tablespoons olive oil
1 teaspoon
    garlic powder
2 fresh flat-leaf parsley
    sprigs, minced
Salt and pepper,
    to taste

Cutting board
Knife (chef's)
Medium mixing bowl
Measuring cups
    and spoons
Medium saucepan
Spatula

MAINS FOR ONE

CILANTRO LIME QUINOA BOWL

30-MINUTE MEAL, NUT-FREE, SOY-FREE
SERVES: 1 • **PREP TIME:** 5 minutes • **COOK TIME:** 20 minutes

This recipe offers a unique flavor combination that includes lime, turmeric, cilantro, and garlic. These flavors come together to create a citrusy yet earthy taste on top of filling, fluffy quinoa. Turmeric not only lends this recipe a cheery yellow color, but it is also known to be one of the most potent anti-oxidant sources. This quinoa bowl goes great with veggie tacos or burritos or any other veggie-forward Mexican dish.

INGREDIENTS

1 cup uncooked
    quinoa
1 garlic clove, minced
¼ red onion, diced
2 tablespoons
    chopped fresh
    cilantro
Juice of 1 lime
1 teaspoon olive oil
1 teaspoon turmeric
2 cups baby spinach
¼ cup crumbled
    feta cheese
Salt and pepper,
    to taste

TOOLS

Colander
Cutting board
Knives (chef's
    and paring)
Measuring cups
    and spoons
Medium saucepan
Medium mixing bowl
Spatula

1. In a medium saucepan, cook the quinoa according to the package directions.
2. While the quinoa cooks, on a cutting board, use a paring knife to mince the garlic. Use a chef's knife to dice the red onion, chop the cilantro, and halve the lime.
3. Drain the cooked quinoa in a colander and place it in a medium mixing bowl. Set aside.
4. In the same saucepan over medium heat, heat the olive oil and sauté the garlic and onion for 3 to 4 minutes.
5. Squeeze out as much juice as you can from the lime into the pan. Add the quinoa, turmeric, spinach, and feta cheese, stirring with a spatula to combine.

6. Cook the quinoa mixture over medium heat, stirring occasionally until the spinach is wilted and the cheese starts to melt, 5 to 7 minutes.

7. Transfer to a serving bowl, season with salt and pepper, top with the cilantro, and enjoy!

INGREDIENT TIP: Quinoa is the holy grail of gluten-free grains. It is actually a seed that becomes quite fluffy when cooked, resembling rice or grains. It has an impressive nutritional profile and is a wonderful source of protein, iron, B vitamins, and fiber. It is also the most common gluten-free option for any recipes that call for rice or grains (there is even pasta made out of quinoa!).

GARDEN PASTA

30-MINUTE MEAL, NUT-FREE, SOY-FREE
SERVES: 1 • **PREP TIME:** 10 minutes • **COOK TIME:** 25 minutes

INGREDIENTS

8 ounces uncooked
    whole-grain
    penne pasta
1 garlic clove, minced
1 zucchini, sliced
½ cup chopped white
    button mushrooms
1 teaspoon olive oil
1 teaspoon Italian
    seasoning
1 (15-ounce) can
    diced tomatoes
½ cup shredded
    mozzarella
    cheese
Salt and pepper,
    to taste

TOOLS

Colander
Cutting board
Knives (paring
    and chef's)
Measuring cups
    and spoons
Medium saucepan
Wooden spoon

This is an ideal dish for when you have a bunch of random vegetables in your refrigerator that you do not know what to do with. If you have mozzarella cheese, pasta, and tomatoes on hand, you can really toss in any kind of vegetables you please. In this version, we are using mushrooms and zucchini to create a hearty pasta dish with nutritional kick.

1. In a medium saucepan, cook the pasta according to the package directions.

2. While the pasta cooks, on a cutting board, use a paring knife to mince the garlic. Use a chef's knife to slice the zucchini and chop the mushrooms.

3. Drain the cooked pasta in a colander and set aside.

4. In the same saucepan over medium heat, heat the olive oil and sauté the garlic for 3 minutes.

5. Add the zucchini and mushrooms, and sauté about 7 minutes, stirring occasionally with a wooden spoon, until the vegetables start to become tender.

6. Add the Italian seasoning and diced tomatoes to the pan, and cook for another 5 minutes, until the seasoning becomes fragrant.

7. Add the pasta back into the pan, along with the mozzarella, and continue cooking and stirring for another 3 to 4 minutes, or until the cheese starts to melt.

8. Season with salt and pepper, transfer to a serving bowl, and enjoy.

EASY CHEDDAR FETTUCCINE ALFREDO

30-MINUTE MEAL, NUT-FREE, SOY-FREE

SERVES: 1 • **PREP TIME:** 5 minutes • **COOK TIME:** 25 minutes

There is something about cheesy Alfredo sauce that makes me drool on demand. This easy-to-make pasta recipe highlights this Italian favorite, because sometimes you want to make something a bit fancier than your typical mac and cheese. This dish tastes delicious when reheated, so do not fret if you have leftovers!

1. In a medium saucepan, cook the pasta according to the package directions.

2. While the pasta cooks, on a cutting board, use a paring knife to mince the garlic.

3. Drain the cooked pasta in a colander and set aside.

4. In the same saucepan used to cook the pasta, heat the olive oil over medium heat and sauté the garlic for 3 minutes.

5. Add the heavy cream, cheddar cheese, mozzarella, onion powder, and flour. Stir well with a wooden spoon until the combination starts to create a sauce. Add a few tablespoons of water or vegetable broth if the sauce becomes too thick. Season with salt and pepper.

6. Turn the heat off and add the pasta back into the saucepan. Toss the pasta and sauce together until they are well combined, and serve.

2 ounces uncooked fettuccine pasta
1 garlic clove, minced
2 tablespoons olive oil
⅓ cup heavy cream
⅓ cup shredded sharp white cheddar cheese
½ cup shredded mozzarella cheese
½ teaspoon onion powder
2 tablespoons flour
Salt and pepper, to taste

Colander
Cutting board
Knife (paring)
Measuring cups and spoons
Medium saucepan
Wooden spoon

RICED CAULIFLOWER BLACK BEAN BOWL

30-MINUTE MEAL, DAIRY-FREE, GLUTEN-FREE, SOY-FREE, VEGAN
SERVES: 1 • **PREP TIME:** 5 minutes • **COOK TIME:** 10 minutes

Craving Mexican? This riced cauliflower black bean bowl is loaded with good-for-you ingredients that will make you feel totally satisfied. It is an easy-peasy, one-pot recipe that can be whipped up in a jiffy and gobbled down even faster.

INGREDIENTS

½ small head
   cauliflower, riced
½ avocado, peeled,
   pitted, and sliced
Juice of ½ lime
1 garlic clove, chopped
1 scallion, sliced
½ (15-ounce) can
   pinto beans, rinsed
   and drained
½ tablespoon olive oil
¼ teaspoon
   ground cumin
Salt and pepper,
   to taste

TOOLS

Cutting board
Cheese grater
Knives (chef's
   and paring)
Measuring spoons
Mixing bowl
Nonstick pan
Spatula

1. On a cutting board, use a chef's knife to cut the leaves off the cauliflower; peel, pit, and slice the avocado (see Kitchen Hack on page 19); and halve a lime. Use a paring knife to chop the garlic and slice the scallion. Rinse and drain the pinto beans and set aside.

2. Use a cheese grater to roughly grate the cauliflower into a mixing bowl so that it crumbles and breaks into "rice."

3. In a nonstick pan over medium-high heat, heat the olive oil and sauté the riced cauliflower for 2 minutes, stirring with a spatula.

4. Squeeze out as much juice as you can from half the lime into the pan. Add the garlic, scallion, cumin, salt, and pepper, and sauté for 2 to 3 minutes more.

5. Transfer your fiesta concoction to a serving bowl, add the black beans and avocado, and serve.

KITCHEN HACK: Riced cauliflower has become so popular that if you don't feel like grating it yourself at home, you can now find it in the produce or frozen aisle of almost any grocery store.

MEDITERRANEAN PITA

30-MINUTE MEAL, NUT-FREE, SOY-FREE
SERVES: 1 • **PREP TIME:** 15 minutes

This lunchtime recipe brings together a bunch of fantastic Mediterranean flavors, such as hummus, kalamata olives, and fresh dill. Most of the work for this pita recipe merely involves chopping your veggies and piling them all on top of the pita. You might have to fend off your family when you sit down to eat it, as they may want to steal this ultra-yummy meal!

1. On a cutting board, use a serrated knife to dice the tomato. Use a chef's knife to chop the cucumber, dill, and romaine lettuce.

2. In a large mixing bowl, combine the tomato, olive oil, balsamic vinegar, cucumber, olives, and dill.

3. Place the pita on a plate, and use a spoon to spread the hummus out on half of the pita.

4. Add the chopped romaine on top of the hummus, and then add the vegetable mixture on top of the romaine. Sprinkle the feta on top, along with a drizzle of olive oil and vinegar.

5. Roll the pita up to create a wrap, and serve!

1 medium tomato, diced
¼ cup chopped cucumber
½ teaspoon chopped fresh dill
½ cup chopped romaine lettuce
1 tablespoon olive oil, plus more to taste
1 teaspoon balsamic vinegar, plus more to taste
4 kalamata olives
1 pita
2 tablespoons hummus
3 tablespoons crumbled feta cheese

Cutting board
Knives (chef's and serrated)
Large mixing bowl
Measuring cups and spoons
Spoon

RANCHERO WRAP

30-MINUTE MEAL, NUT-FREE, SOY-FREE
SERVES: 1 • **PREP TIME:** 15 minutes

INGREDIENTS

1 carrot, peeled and
    cut into strips
½ orange bell pepper,
    seeded and cut
    into 4 strips
Handful spinach,
    chopped
½ cup shredded
    broccoli
1 tortilla
2 tablespoons
    ranch dressing
2 slices
    American cheese

TOOLS

Cutting board
Knife (chef's)
Handheld grater
Measuring cups
    and spoons
Spoon
Vegetable peeler

Ranch dressing was a favorite with a lot of my meals growing up, and I am certain it is one of your favorites, too. This ranch-filled wrap comes together in 15 minutes or less and boasts colorful vegetables and good old American cheese. Since ranch dressing can be high in calories and fat, I always make sure to balance this indulgent dressing with lots of nutritious vegetables!

1. On a cutting board, use a vegetable peeler to peel the carrot. Use a chef's knife to cut the carrot into strips, seed and cut the bell pepper into 4 strips (see Kitchen Hack on page 42), and chop the spinach. Use a handheld grater to shred the broccoli.

2. Place the tortilla on a plate. Use a spoon to spread the ranch dressing on half of the tortilla. Add the bell pepper, spinach, carrot, and broccoli on top of the ranch, and then place the two slices of American cheese on top of the vegetables.

3. Roll up the tortilla to create a wrap, and serve!

CHEESY VEGGIE QUESADILLA

30-MINUTE MEAL, NUT-FREE, SOY-FREE
SERVES: 1 • **PREP TIME:** 5 minutes • **COOK TIME:** 15 minutes

This cheese-filled veggie quesadilla is seriously addicting, especially when served fresh off the skillet. The mix of mushrooms, tomatoes, and zucchini pairs beautifully with the southwestern blend of chili powder and cumin.

1. On a cutting board, use a chef's knife to dice the onion, mushrooms, and zucchini. Use a paring knife to mince the garlic. Use a serrated knife to dice the tomatoes.

2. In a nonstick pan over medium heat, heat the olive oil and sauté the onion and garlic for 3 minutes.

3. Add the tomatoes, mushrooms, zucchini, chili powder, and cumin, and continue sautéing for 5 to 7 minutes, until the vegetables start to become tender.

4. In a separate nonstick pan, add 1 tortilla. Top the tortilla with half of the cheese, the cooked vegetables, and then the rest of the cheese.

5. Place the other tortilla on top and cook the quesadilla over medium heat on each side for about 3 minutes, flipping it with a spatula.

6. Remove the quesadilla from the heat, place it on a plate, top it with the sour cream, and enjoy.

KITCHEN HACK: Want to bake your quesadilla instead? Simply heat the oven to 400°F, prepare a quesadilla on a greased baking sheet, and bake it for about 10 minutes, or until the cheese starts to melt.

¼ white onion, diced
4 mushrooms, diced
½ zucchini, diced
1 garlic clove, minced
2 tomatoes, diced
1 tablespoon olive oil
½ teaspoon
    chili powder
½ teaspoon cumin
2 tortillas
½ cup shredded Monterey Jack cheese
2 tablespoons
    sour cream

Cutting board
Knives (chef's, paring,
    and serrated)
Measuring cups
    and spoons
Nonstick pans (2)
Spatula

EGG & VEGETABLES FRIED RICE

30-MINUTE MEAL, DAIRY-FREE, NUT-FREE, VEGAN
SERVES: 1 • **PREP TIME:** 5 minutes • **COOK TIME:** 15 minutes

INGREDIENTS

1 cup uncooked
    white rice
1 egg
1 teaspoon sesame
    oil, divided
1 garlic clove, minced
1 scallion, diced
¼ cup diced broccoli
¼ cup diced carrot
¼ cup diced
    bell pepper
2 tablespoons
    soy sauce
1 teaspoon
    white pepper

TOOLS

Cutting board
Knives (chef's
    and paring)
Measuring cups
    and spoons
Nonstick pan
Saucepan
Small mixing bowls (2)
Spatula
Whisk

This is an essential weeknight meal that you can quickly cook and eat either as an entrée or as a side dish to spring rolls or a big leafy salad. It can be made without egg, and you can use riced cauliflower in place of regular rice if you are on a cauliflower kick.

1. In a saucepan, cook the rice according to the package directions.

2. Meanwhile, in a small mixing bowl, whisk the egg until the yolk and white are blended well.

3. In a nonstick pan over medium heat, heat ½ teaspoon of sesame oil and use a spatula to scramble the egg for about 1 minute. Transfer to a separate small bowl and set aside.

4. On a cutting board, use a paring knife to mince the garlic. Use a chef's knife to dice the scallion, broccoli, carrot, and pepper.

5. Reheat the nonstick pan and add the remaining ½ teaspoon of oil to the pan. Sauté the garlic for 3 minutes, then add the broccoli, carrot, bell pepper, soy sauce, and white pepper, letting it cook for 5 more minutes, until the vegetables become tender.

6. Add the cooked rice to the pan and continue cooking, stirring with a spatula until well combined, about another 5 minutes.

7. Add the scrambled egg to the pan, stirring and cooking for another minute. Top the fried rice with the diced scallion and serve.

TEMPEH STIR-FRY

30-MINUTE MEAL, DAIRY-FREE, VEGAN
SERVES: 1 • **PREP TIME:** 10 minutes • **COOK TIME:** 15 minutes

This tempeh stir-fry can be made as a delicious addition to Egg & Vegetables Fried Rice (page 86) or served over steamed rice or quinoa. It is ready in less than 30 minutes and showcases my favorite plant-based source of protein: tempeh. It is definitely a recipe you will want to make in larger quantities for your family, as well!

1. On a cutting board, use a paring knife to mince the garlic, cube the tempeh, dice the scallion, and peel and finely mince the ginger.

2. In a small mixing bowl, whisk together the chili garlic paste, sugar, soy sauce, and 2 teaspoons of sesame oil.

3. Add the tempeh and toss until the tempeh is coated.

4. In a nonstick pan over medium heat, heat the remaining 1 teaspoon of sesame oil and sauté the garlic for 3 minutes.

5. Add the frozen vegetables and cook for 5 more minutes, until they start to become slightly tender.

6. Add the glazed tempeh and sauce from the mixing bowl into the pan and continue cooking for 4 to 5 minutes, or until the tempeh is well cooked.

7. Top with the minced ginger and scallion. Add more soy sauce if needed, and serve.

1 garlic clove, minced
2 ounces tempeh, cubed
1 scallion, diced
1 (¼-inch) piece ginger, peeled and finely minced
1 teaspoon chili garlic paste
1 teaspoon sugar
Soy sauce, to taste (start out with a little and add more as you go)
3 teaspoons sesame oil, divided
1 cup frozen mixed vegetables

Cutting board
Knife (paring)
Measuring cups and spoons
Nonstick pan
Small mixing bowl
Whisk

MAINS FOR ONE

SPAGHETTI SQUASH WITH MUSHROOM BOLOGNESE

GLUTEN-FREE, NUT-FREE, SOY-FREE

SERVES: 1 • **PREP TIME:** 15 minutes • **COOK TIME:** 25 minutes

INGREDIENTS

½ spaghetti squash,
    halved lengthwise
½ white onion, diced
½ cup chopped
    button mushrooms
1 garlic clove, minced
1 tablespoon olive oil
1 (15-ounce) can
    crushed tomatoes
½ teaspoon oregano
Salt and pepper,
    to taste
2 teaspoons
    tomato paste
1 cup shredded
    mozzarella
    cheese, divided
3 fresh basil leaves

TOOLS

Baking dish (at least
    8 inches long)
Cutting board
Fork
Knives (chef's
    and paring)
Measuring cups
    and spoons
Nonstick pan
Spatula

Traditional Bolognese sauce consists of tomatoes, herbs, wine, and minced beef. We are, of course, remixing this to create a lighter, vegetarian version and nixing the wine and beef! This Bolognese sauce calls for a blend of fresh basil, crushed tomatoes, mushrooms (instead of beef), garlic, and oregano. It is simmered to perfection and served on a bed of fresh spaghetti squash. You could say this is the ultimate plant-based meal!

1. On a cutting board, use a chef's knife to halve the squash lengthwise. Store one half in the fridge for later use.
2. Place the other half cut-side down in a ceramic baking dish. Add 1 to 2 inches of water to the dish and microwave it for 10 minutes.
3. While the squash cooks in the microwave, on a cutting board, use the chef's knife to dice the onion and chop the mushrooms. Use a paring knife to mince the garlic.
4. Remove the squash from the microwave. It's done if you can pierce the skin easily with a fork. Set the squash aside to cool.
5. In a nonstick pan over medium heat, heat the olive oil and sauté the onion and garlic for 3 minutes.

6. Add the mushrooms, tomatoes, oregano, salt, and pepper. Using a spatula, stir and cook for 7 to 10 more minutes, or until the mushrooms are tender.

7. Add the tomato paste and ½ cup of mozzarella, and continue cooking until the mozzarella melts in with the other ingredients.

8. Use a fork to scrape the inside of the squash to remove the flesh, which will be stringy and resemble spaghetti. Place 1 to 2 cups in a bowl, and top with the mushroom Bolognese sauce.

9. Sprinkle the remaining ½ cup of mozzarella cheese on top, along with the basil leaves. Serve and enjoy! Store leftovers in an airtight container in the refrigerator.

RANCH GREEN BEAN & POTATO SKILLET

30-MINUTE MEAL, GLUTEN-FREE, NUT-FREE

SERVES: 1 • **PREP TIME:** 5 minutes • **COOK TIME:** 20 minutes

INGREDIENTS

1 medium red potato

¼ white onion, diced

½ (15-ounce) can
French green
beans, rinsed
and drained

2 teaspoons butter

1 teaspoon ranch
dressing, plus more
to taste

½ teaspoon
Italian seasoning

1 teaspoon
garlic powder

Salt and pepper,
to taste

TOOLS

Cutting board

Fork

Knife (chef's)

Measuring spoons

Microwave-safe plate

Nonstick pan

Spatula

This recipe is an appetizing bowl of green bean goodness! I love this meal when I am craving a hearty and comforting snack. Something about the mix of green beans and potato reminds me of a cozy night in during the winter.

1. Poke holes in the potato with a fork. Place it on a microwave-safe plate and cook it in the microwave for 5 minutes. Flip the potato over on the plate and microwave for another 4 minutes.

2. While the potato cooks, on a cutting board, use a chef's knife to dice the onion. Rinse and drain the green beans.

3. In a nonstick pan over medium heat, melt the butter and sauté the onion and green beans for 4 to 5 minutes, stirring occasionally with a spatula.

4. Use the chef's knife to cut the potato into small wedges and add the wedges to the pan, along with the ranch dressing, Italian seasoning, garlic powder, salt, and pepper. Cook for 3 to 5 more minutes, until all the flavors are infused with one another.

5. Remove the pan from the heat, add more ranch dressing if preferred, and serve!

SWEET POTATO NACHOS

GLUTEN-FREE, NUT-FREE, SOY-FREE
SERVES: 1 • **PREP TIME:** 10 minutes • **COOK TIME:** 30 minutes

Nachos for dinner? Yes please! This nacho recipe is a complete meal since it contains all the right types of nutrients: protein, healthy fats, and carbohydrates. Using sweet potatoes instead of tortilla chips really boosts the nutritional value of this dish.

1. Preheat the oven to 400°F. Line a baking sheet with aluminum foil greased with the coconut oil. Set aside.

2. On a cutting board, use a chef's knife to slice the sweet potato. Arrange the slices in an even layer on the prepared baking sheet.

3. Sprinkle the sweet potato slices with the adobo seasoning and chili powder, then bake them for about 18 minutes.

4. While the sweet potato bakes, on a cutting board, use a chef's knife to halve a lime, dice the red onion, and peel, pit, and slice the avocado (see Kitchen Hack on page 19). Rinse and drain the black beans and set aside.

5. Remove the baking sheet from the oven and flip the sweet potato slices with a spatula, then top with the shredded cheese. Return to the oven for another 10 minutes, or until the cheese starts to brown.

6. Transfer the nachos to a serving plate. Squeeze out as much juice as you can from half the lime onto the nachos. Top with the onion, black beans, and avocado. Garnish with pickled jalapeños if desired, and serve.

½ tablespoon coconut oil
1 sweet potato, cut into thin "chips"
½ teaspoon adobo seasoning
½ teaspoon chili powder
Juice of ½ lime
¼ red onion, diced
½ avocado, peeled, pitted, and sliced
½ cup canned black beans, rinsed and drained
½ cup shredded Mexican cheese blend
Pickled sliced jalapeño peppers, for garnish (optional)

Aluminum foil
Baking sheet
Cutting board
Knife (chef's)
Measuring cups and spoons
Spatula

GRILLED PIMENTO CHEESE & TOMATO SANDWICH

5 MAIN INGREDIENTS, 30-MINUTE MEAL, NUT-FREE, SOY-FREE
SERVES: 1 • **PREP TIME:** 5 minutes • **COOK TIME:** 10 minutes

INGREDIENTS

6 slices sharp
   cheddar cheese
2 slices bread
1 vine tomato, sliced
1 tablespoon butter
¼ cup jarred pimentos
Hot sauce, to taste

TOOLS

Cutting board
Knife (serrated)
Measuring cups
   and spoons
Nonstick pan
Spatula

A step up from the standard grilled cheese sandwich, this pimento grilled cheese comes with a kick! It can be served with a refreshing leafy salad or a bowl of tomato soup. It is a flavorsome combination of cheddar cheese, pimento peppers, and hot sauce topped with a fresh sliced tomato all between two crisp slices of bread.

1. Place 3 cheddar cheese slices on each of the bread slices, then set them aside.

2. On a cutting board, use a serrated knife to slice the tomato.

3. In a nonstick pan over medium heat, melt the butter. Place both pieces of bread in the pan, with the cheese sides facing up. Cook for a few minutes, until the cheese starts to melt.

4. Top one slice of bread with the jarred pimentos and tomato slices. Shake some hot sauce onto the tomato slices. Then, use a spatula to flip the other piece of bread on top, so the two cheese sides come together.

5. Continue to cook the sandwich for 30 seconds to 1 minute, then remove it from the heat. Let it cool for a few minutes before serving.

KITCHEN HACK: Want to save even more time on this recipe? A lot of stores carry premade pimento cheese spread that can be slathered on your sandwich in lieu of starting from scratch with cheese slices and jarred pimentos. Don't forget to read the labels to make sure the cheese is vegetarian friendly!

GARLIC TOFU BOWL

DAIRY-FREE, VEGAN

SERVES: 1 • **PREP TIME:** 20 minutes • **COOK TIME:** 20 minutes

This filling combo of brown rice, tofu, sriracha sauce, and fresh green vegetables is the perfect blend when you want to cook up a full meal served in a bowl. I suggest doubling this recipe so that you can have leftovers for lunch the next day. This dish is bursting with spicy and sweet flavor and is a good one to try if you're new to eating tofu.

1. Wrap the tofu in a few paper towels and press on it to remove any excess liquid (this helps the tofu infuse with the flavors you use in your cooking).

2. On a cutting board, use a chef's knife to dice the tofu into bite-size pieces, chop the spinach and broccolini, and halve a lime. Use a paring knife to mince the garlic.

3. In a medium mixing bowl, squeeze out as much juice as you can from half the lime. Add the sriracha, rice vinegar, sugar, tofu, and a drizzle of soy sauce, tossing so that the tofu is fully coated. Let the mixture sit for 10 to 15 minutes.

4. Meanwhile, in a medium saucepan, cook the rice according to the package directions. Transfer the cooked rice to a small mixing bowl and set aside.

5. In the same saucepan used to cook the rice, heat the sesame oil over medium heat and sauté the garlic for 3 minutes.

3 ounces firm tofu, drained and diced
1 cup chopped spinach
½ cup chopped broccolini
Juice of ½ lime
1 garlic clove, minced
½ tablespoon sriracha
¼ teaspoon rice vinegar
¼ tablespoon sugar
Soy sauce, to taste
1 cup uncooked brown rice
1 teaspoon sesame oil

Cutting board
Knife (chef's)
Measuring cups and spoons
Medium mixing bowl
Medium saucepan
Paper towels
Small mixing bowl

(CONTINUED)

MAINS FOR ONE

Garlic Tofu Bowl

6. Add the tofu mixture and broccolini to the saucepan, and continue cooking for 7 minutes, or until the broccolini starts to become tender.

7. Add the rice and spinach, and continue cooking until the spinach wilts.

8. Transfer to a serving bowl, drizzle more soy sauce on top as desired, and enjoy.

MIX IT UP: Broccolini is a cousin of broccoli. You can tell the difference by the length of its stem (broccolini is longer). It has a milder flavor than broccoli, making it a great addition to a quick stir-fry recipe. Broccolini can be sautéed, grilled, or roasted to create a simple side dish. All it really needs is a dash of salt and a splash of oil to bring out its flavor.

PIZZA SKILLET

30-MINUTE MEAL, GLUTEN-FREE, NUT-FREE, SOY-FREE
SERVES: 1 • **PREP TIME:** 5 minutes • **COOK TIME:** 25 minutes

If you are craving a pizza but do not feel like going all out with buying or making a crust, this pizza skillet recipe has got you covered! Using only one skillet, you will combine peppers, artichoke hearts, olives, and mushrooms with zesty marinara sauce and mozzarella cheese for a crustless pizza that can be eaten by itself or on top of a grilled flatbread.

1. On a cutting board, use a chef's knife to slice the white onion, mushrooms, bell pepper (see Kitchen Hack on page 42), and black olives. Chop the baby spinach. Rinse and drain the artichoke hearts and set aside.

2. In a cast-iron skillet over medium heat, heat the olive oil and sauté the onion for 3 minutes, stirring with a spatula.

3. Add the mushrooms, bell pepper, artichoke hearts, and Italian seasoning. Continue cooking for 5 to 7 minutes, or until the vegetables start to become tender.

4. Add the spinach, black olives, and marinara sauce, and continue cooking until the spinach wilts.

5. Sprinkle the mozzarella cheese on top, lower the heat to medium-low, cover the pan, and cook until the cheese melts.

6. Remove the skillet from the heat, and serve.

¼ small white onion, sliced
¼ cup white button mushrooms, sliced
¼ cup sliced green bell pepper
5 black olives, sliced
1 cup baby spinach, chopped
¼ cup canned artichoke hearts, rinsed and drained
2 teaspoons olive oil
½ teaspoon Italian seasoning
¼ cup marinara sauce
½ cup shredded mozzarella cheese

Cast-iron skillet
Cutting board
Knife (chef's)
Measuring cups and spoons
Spatula

ASIAGO WHITE-BEAN POLENTA SKILLET

GLUTEN-FREE, NUT-FREE, SOY-FREE
SERVES: 1 • **PREP TIME:** 10 minutes • **COOK TIME:** 40 minutes

INGREDIENTS

1 garlic clove, minced
¼ yellow onion, diced
3 kale leaves, chopped
1 medium vine
    tomato, chopped
½ (15-ounce) can can-
    nellini beans, rinsed
    and drained
4 cups water
1 cup polenta
1 tablespoon olive oil
1 teaspoon
    Italian seasoning
½ cup shredded
    Asiago cheese
Chopped fresh parsley,
    for garnish

TOOLS

Cutting board
Knives (chef's, paring,
    and serrated)
Large saucepan
Measuring cups
    and spoons
Nonstick pan
Wooden spoon

This recipe calls for ingredients that may already be in your pantry. It is the ideal meal for when you are craving the flavors of Italy, and the blend of polenta, beans, and kale will definitely fill you up! Plus, this recipe tastes even better the next day, when all of the flavors have had time to infuse together in the fridge, so you can make extra for hassle-free eating tomorrow!

1. On a cutting board, use a paring knife to mince the garlic. Use a chef's knife to dice the onion and chop the kale. Use a serrated knife to chop the tomato. Rinse and drain the cannellini beans and set aside.

2. Add the water to a large saucepan and bring to a boil. Pour in the polenta while gently stirring with a wooden spoon at the same time. This will help prevent the polenta from clumping. Reduce the heat and let the water simmer to thicken the polenta.

3. Cover the pan and continue simmering for about 30 minutes. Stir the polenta every so often to prevent clumps from forming. Remove from the heat once the polenta is thick and fluffy.

4. Meanwhile, in a nonstick pan over medium heat, heat the olive oil and sauté the garlic and onion for 3 minutes.

5. Add the kale and Italian seasoning, and cook for 10 to 15 minutes, or until the kale starts to wilt.

6. Add the tomato, beans, and Asiago, and continue cooking for another 5 minutes.

7. Transfer the polenta to a serving bowl and top it with the vegetable and cheese mixture. You can also mix them together in the bowl to combine the flavors. Garnish with parsley and serve.

TORTILLA PIZZA

30-MINUTE MEAL, NUT-FREE, SOY-FREE
SERVES: 1 • **PREP TIME:** 10 minutes • **COOK TIME:** 15 minutes

INGREDIENTS

3 small
   tomatoes, sliced
5 green olives, sliced
¼ red onion, sliced
1 tortilla
½ cup shredded
   mozzarella cheese
1 teaspoon dried basil

TOOLS

Baking sheet
Cutting board
Knives (chef's, paring,
   and serrated)
Measuring cups
   and spoons
Parchment paper

Want to make a pizza but don't have dough on hand? You can create one with a tortilla instead! Tortilla pizzas are the perfect meal for one, since a tortilla makes an ideal single serving. All you have to do is add the toppings of your choice to a tortilla, pop it in the oven, and 15 minutes later, you'll have a crispy pizza ready to be devoured.

1. Preheat the oven to 375°F. Line a baking sheet with parchment paper and set aside.
2. On a cutting board, use a serrated knife to slice the tomatoes. Use a paring knife to slice the green olives. Use a chef's knife to slice the red onion.
3. Place the tortilla on the prepared baking sheet and top it with the sliced tomatoes, olives, and red onion.
4. Evenly sprinkle the mozzarella on top. Top the pizza with the dried basil.
5. Bake for about 15 minutes, or until the cheese has melted and the tortilla looks crisp and golden.

MIX IT UP: The wonderful thing about making pizzas is that you can add a wide variety of toppings. You can load up on the veggies to create a vegetable-forward variety, use a blend of three cheeses for added flavor, or go heavy on the onion and garlic to make an extra-aromatic dish. The more you make, the more ideas you will come up with!

STOVETOP ENCHILADAS

NUT-FREE, SOY-FREE
SERVES: 1 • **PREP TIME:** 10 minutes • **COOK TIME:** 30 minutes

Typically, enchiladas are baked in the oven, but we are fast-tracking this recipe by creating a skillet version. This way, you use fewer utensils and less kitchen equipment so there is barely any cleanup.

1. On a cutting board, use a chef's knife to dice the white onion. Use a paring knife to mince the garlic. Drain the canned tomatoes, and rinse and drain the pinto beans. Set aside.

2. In a cast-iron skillet over medium heat, heat the olive oil and sauté the onion and garlic for 3 minutes, stirring with a spatula.

3. Add the tomatoes, frozen bell peppers, chili powder, and cumin, and continue cooking for 10 minutes.

4. Add the pinto beans, enchilada sauce, and tortilla pieces, and cook for another 10 minutes.

5. Top with the cheese, turn the heat down, and cover the pan. Let it cook for 3 more minutes.

6. Remove the skillet from the stovetop, garnish with toppings of your choice, and serve.

¼ white onion, diced
1 garlic clove, minced
½ (15-ounce) can diced tomatoes, drained
¼ cup canned pinto beans, rinsed and drained
1 tablespoon olive oil
½ cup frozen bell pepper blend
1 teaspoon chili powder
¼ teaspoon cumin
1 tablespoon enchilada sauce
1 tortilla, chopped into large pieces
½ cup shredded Mexican cheese blend

Cast-iron skillet
Cutting board
Knives (chef's and paring)
Measuring cups and spoons
Spatula

LOADED
VEGGIE
PIZZA,
PAGE 103

chapter 6
MEALS FOR FRIENDS & FAMILY

The delicious flavors of these larger meals are sure to impress your friends and family, whether they are fellow vegetarians, curious about plant-based eating, or die-hard meat eaters.

GREEK BAGUETTE PIZZA BITES

NUT-FREE, SOY-FREE
MAKES: 12 bites (2 bites per serving) • **PREP TIME:** 20 minutes •
COOK TIME: 15 minutes

(see Kitchen Hack on page 42)

INGREDIENTS

Olive oil, for greasing,
   plus ½ tablespoon
3 garlic cloves, minced
1 French baguette,
   halved lengthwise
½ cup sliced green
   bell pepper
2 medium red
   onions, sliced
½ cup kalamata
   olives, diced
3 medium
   tomatoes, sliced
½ teaspoon
   Italian seasoning
1½ cups crumbled
   feta cheese

TOOLS

Baking sheet
Cutting board
Knives (chef's, paring,
   and serrated)
Measuring cups
   and spoons

These baguette pizza bites are a definite party pleaser, with a rich and salty blend of Mediterranean ingredients that create a burst of vibrant flavor in every bite. This recipe is a creative way to transform a baguette loaf into mini pizza bites, and it only takes 30 minutes from start to finish!

1. Preheat the oven to 400°F. Grease a baking sheet with olive oil and set aside.

2. On a cutting board, use a paring knife to mince the garlic. Use a chef's knife to halve the baguette lengthwise, slice the bell pepper (see Kitchen Hack on page 42), slice the red onions, and dice the olives. Use a serrated knife to slice the tomatoes.

3. Place the baguette halves, cut-side up, on the prepared baking sheet. Add the tomatoes, garlic, bell pepper, olives, Italian seasoning, onion slices, and feta cheese on top. Drizzle with the remaining ½ teaspoon olive oil and bake for 10 to 15 minutes, or until the cheese has completely melted.

4. Once done, cut the baguette into bite-size pieces, and serve.

MIX IT UP: If you have all the other ingredients on hand but do not have a baguette, feel free to get creative! You can also make single-serve mini pizzas on English muffins. The end result will be very similar.

LOADED VEGGIE PIZZA

30-MINUTE MEAL, NUT-FREE, SOY-FREE
SERVES: 4 to 6 • **PREP TIME:** 10 minutes • **COOK TIME:** 20 minutes

Homemade pizzas are usually way healthier than the store-bought varieties, because there is significantly less sodium in each serving. It is also super fun to make pizzas at home and go all out with whatever types of toppings you desire. This specific recipe calls for a hearty blend of olives, artichoke hearts, spinach, and zucchini topped with tons of melty mozzarella cheese.

1. Preheat the oven to 450°F.

2. On a cutting board, use a chef's knife to slice the onion and zucchini and to chop the spinach. Drain and rinse the artichoke hearts.

3. Place the pizza crust on a pizza pan or baking sheet. Spread the tomato sauce evenly over the pizza crust.

4. Arrange the olives, onion, artichoke hearts, zucchini, and spinach on the crust, aiming for even distribution of the ingredients.

5. Add the cheese on top, followed by the oregano and parsley.

6. Bake for 15 to 20 minutes, or until the cheese has melted and the edges of the pizza are golden brown.

1 white onion, sliced
1 zucchini, sliced
3 cups chopped
   spinach
1 (15-ounce) can
   artichoke hearts,
   rinsed and drained
1 (8-ounce) can
   tomato sauce
1 prebaked
   store-bought
   pizza crust
¼ cup green olives
1¼ cup shredded
   mozzarella cheese
1 teaspoon oregano
1 teaspoon parsley

Cutting board
Knife (chef's)
Measuring cups
   and spoons
Pizza pan or
   baking sheet

HOMEMADE MACARONI

30-MINUTE MEAL, SOY-FREE

SERVES: 6 • **PREP TIME:** 5 minutes • **COOK TIME:** 20 minutes

INGREDIENTS

3 cups uncooked
    elbow macaroni
3 tablespoons butter
3 tablespoons
    almond flour
¼ tablespoon
    smoked paprika
2 cups unsweetened
    almond milk
¼ cup sour cream
2 cups shredded sharp
    cheddar cheese
1 cup shredded
    smoked Gouda
    cheese
Salt and pepper,
    to taste
Panko bread crumbs,
    for garnish

TOOLS

Colander
Large pot
Measuring cups
    and spoons
Whisk
Wooden spoon

Say goodbye to packaged mac and cheese and hello to this simple yet delicious homemade alternative. This is my favorite mac and cheese recipe because it is overflowing with creamy cheese and topped with crunchy crumbs. The Gouda and dash of paprika add a hearty smokiness. It is hands down a cheese lover's dream!

1. Preheat the oven to 350°F.
2. In a large pot, cook the pasta according to the package directions. Drain the cooked pasta in a colander.
3. In the same pot that you cooked the pasta in, melt the butter over medium heat. Add the flour, paprika, and almond milk, whisking to combine.
4. Add the sour cream and continue whisking until the sauce thickens a bit, then turn the heat to low and add the cheddar and Gouda cheeses. Continue whisking to mix all ingredients together.
5. Add the pasta back to the pot and stir with a wooden spoon until the pasta is evenly coated in sauce. Add salt and pepper to taste, and continue stirring to combine.
6. Transfer the mac and cheese to serving dishes and garnish it with bread crumbs.

CAULIFLOWER COCONUT CURRY

30-MINUTE MEAL, DAIRY-FREE, GLUTEN-FREE, SOY-FREE, VEGAN
SERVES: 4 • **PREP TIME:** 5 minutes • **COOK TIME:** 25 minutes

Curry recipes are a staple not only in Indian cuisine but also in cultures all around the world. This cauliflower coconut curry is created in one pot and is completely vegan, gluten-free, and soy-free. Its robust flavor comes from a blend of turmeric, ginger, garlic, and curry. Not only will this recipe delight all of your senses, but it will give you a serving of healthy vegetables, too!

1. On a cutting board, use a chef's knife to remove the outer leaves of the cauliflower and chop it into florets. Use a paring knife to dice the onion, mince the garlic and ginger, and dice the carrots. Drain and rinse the green beans and set aside.

2. In a pot over medium heat, heat 1 tablespoon of vegetable broth. Add the onion, ginger, and garlic, stirring with a wooden spoon, and cook for 3 minutes. Then add the curry powder and turmeric, and continue stirring.

3. Add the coconut milk, cauliflower, carrots, green beans, and the remaining 3 cups of vegetable broth, and bring to a boil. Once boiling, reduce the heat and simmer the curry for about 20 minutes.

4. Season with salt and pepper, and serve.

KITCHEN HACK: Curry dishes pair wonderfully with quinoa and rice, and can be garnished with cilantro or lime juice. You can never go wrong with a curry dish, as the blend of flavors works well with virtually any type of vegetable!

1 small head
    cauliflower,
    chopped
1 medium yellow
    onion, diced
3 garlic cloves, minced
1 tablespoon minced
    fresh ginger
3 large carrots, diced
1 cup canned green
    beans, rinsed
    and drained
1 tablespoon veg-
    etable broth,
    plus 3 cups
1 teaspoon
    curry powder
½ teaspoon turmeric
1 (15-ounce) can
    coconut milk
Salt and pepper,
    to taste

Cutting board
Knives (paring
    and chef's)
Measuring cups
    and spoons
Pot
Wooden spoon

STOVETOP BEAN FAJITAS

30-MINUTE MEAL, DAIRY-FREE, NUT-FREE, SOY-FREE, VEGAN
SERVES: 4 • **PREP TIME:** 5 minutes • **COOK TIME:** 10 minutes

INGREDIENTS

1 medium yellow
    onion, diced
Juice of 1 lime
2 avocados, peeled,
    pitted, and sliced
3 garlic cloves, minced
1 (15-ounce) can
    pinto beans, rinsed
    and drained
1 tablespoon olive oil
½ cup frozen mixed
    bell peppers
1 teaspoon cumin
1 teaspoon
    chili powder
8 corn tortillas

TOOLS

Cutting board
Knives (chef's
    and paring)
Measuring cups
    and spoons
Nonstick pan
Spatula

These fajitas provide a flavorful combination of pinto beans, bell peppers, warming spices, and creamy avocado. The best part? They take only 15 minutes to make! These can be served with cilantro rice, Guacamole (page 56), and even Veggie-Packed Tortilla Soup (page 46) for the ultimate Mexican-inspired, plant-based meal.

1. On a cutting board, Use a chef's knife to dice the onion, halve the lime, and peel, pit, and slice the avocados (see Kitchen Hack on page 19). Use a paring knife to mince the garlic. Drain and rinse the pinto beans and set aside.

2. In a nonstick pan over medium heat, heat the olive oil and sauté the onion and garlic for 3 minutes, stirring with a spatula.

3. Add the mixed bell peppers to the pan and cook until fully defrosted.

4. Squeeze out as much juice as you can from the lime into the pan. Add the pinto beans, cumin, and chili powder, and continue cooking for 5 more minutes.

5. Warm the tortillas for 30 seconds or so in the microwave. Top each warm tortilla with the fajita mixture. Garnish with slices of avocado, and serve!

QUINOA BURRITO BOWL BAKE

NUT-FREE, SOY-FREE
SERVES: 4 • **PREP TIME:** 10 minutes • **COOK TIME:** 40 minutes

This gluten-free quinoa bake is created by simply cooking up a batch of quinoa, throwing all of the ingredients together in a bowl, and baking the mixture into a garlicky, spicy casserole. It is a wonderful recipe to make when having friends over for a movie night or even for Sunday dinner with your family. You can also easily save leftovers for school the next day.

1. Preheat the oven to 350°F. Grease a baking dish with cooking spray and set aside.

2. In a medium saucepan, bring the vegetable broth to a boil. Add the quinoa, then reduce the heat to a simmer. Allow the quinoa to cook in the pot, covered, for 15 minutes, or until it looks fluffy.

3. While the quinoa is cooking, rinse and drain the black beans and kidney beans and place them in a large mixing bowl.

4. Add the cooked quinoa, ½ cup of cheese, green chiles, diced tomatoes, garlic powder, and chili powder, mixing well with a spatula or wooden spoon to combine.

5. Transfer the mixture to the prepared baking dish and top it with the remaining ½ cup of cheese. Bake for 25 minutes, or until the cheese has browned on top.

6. Remove from the oven and allow it to cool a bit before serving.

Nonstick
    cooking spray
2 cups vegetable broth
1 cup uncooked
    quinoa
1 (15-ounce) can
    black beans, rinsed
    and drained
1 (15-ounce) can red
    kidney beans,
    rinsed and drained
1 cup shredded
    Colby Jack
    cheese, divided
1 (7-ounce) can
    green chiles
1 (15-ounce) can
    diced tomatoes
2 teaspoons
    garlic powder
2 tablespoons
    chili powder

Baking dish
Large mixing bowl
Measuring cups
    and spoons
Medium saucepan
Spatula or
    wooden spoon

RICE NOODLE RAMEN

30-MINUTE MEAL, DAIRY-FREE, NUT-FREE, VEGAN
SERVES: 4 • **PREP TIME:** 5 minutes • **COOK TIME:** 15 minutes

INGREDIENTS

1 pound uncooked
   rice noodles
1 (1-inch) piece ginger,
   peeled and minced
4 garlic cloves, minced
8 ounces mushrooms,
   diced
3 heads baby bok
   choy, sliced
Chopped scallions, for
   topping (optional)
Chopped tofu, for
   topping (optional)
Chopped hard-boiled
   egg, for topping
   (optional)
1 tablespoon
   sesame oil
6 cups vegetable broth
2 tablespoons white
   miso paste

TOOLS

Colander
Cutting board
Knives (chef's
   and paring)
Large bowl
Large saucepan
Measuring cups
   and spoons
Pot
Spatula

Ramen is one of my favorite bowls to slurp up when I want to feel extra snug. It is quick and simple to make, and you can have fun with your toppings and ingredients of choice. There are so many different ways to make ramen. Once you perfect this basic version, who knows what else you will come up with!

1. Bring a pot of water to a boil, and cook the rice noodles according to the package directions.

2. While the noodles cook, on a cutting board, use a paring knife to peel and mince the ginger and mince the garlic. Use a chef's knife to dice the mushrooms, slice the bok choy, and chop the scallion, tofu, or hard-boiled egg, if using.

3. Drain the cooked noodles in a colander. Transfer them to a large bowl and set aside.

4. Meanwhile, in a large saucepan over medium heat, heat the sesame oil and sauté the garlic and ginger for 3 minutes, stirring constantly with a spatula.

5. Add the mushrooms, bok choy, vegetable broth, and white miso paste, and continue to cook, stirring occasionally, until the mixture comes to a boil. Reduce the heat and let simmer for 7 to 10 minutes.

6. Stir in the cooked rice noodles, and cook everything together for another 3 minutes.

7. Transfer the ramen to serving bowls. If you'd like, top it with the chopped scallions, tofu, or egg, and enjoy!

DID YOU KNOW? There are at least 22 versions of ramen in Japan! A huge variety of different flavor combinations is possible, depending on the toppings, noodles, and broths that are brought together. This makes for a great reason to experiment with different flavors in the kitchen!

GRAIN-FREE ZUCCHINI LASAGNA

GLUTEN-FREE, NUT-FREE, SOY-FREE
SERVES: 4 to 6 • **PREP TIME:** 15 minutes • **COOK TIME:** 45 minutes

INGREDIENTS

Nonstick
    cooking spray
1 medium onion, diced
4 medium zucchini,
    sliced lengthwise
    into thin strips
½ cup ricotta cheese
2 cups shredded
    mozzarella
    cheese, divided
1 egg
1 tablespoon olive oil
2 tablespoons
    Italian seasoning
2 teaspoons
    garlic powder
3 cups marinara
    sauce, divided

TOOLS

Baking dish
Cutting board
Knife (chef's)
Measuring cups
    and spoons
Medium mixing bowl
Paper towels
Spatula

Did you know that you can make lasagna without the actual lasagna noodles? Here, we are using zucchini instead of pasta to create healthy layers without sacrificing taste. It's still just as cheesy as the traditional recipe and tastes almost identical, but without any grains!

1. Preheat the oven to 350°F. Grease a baking dish with cooking spray and set aside.

2. On a cutting board, use a chef's knife to dice the onion and slice the zucchini lengthwise into strips. Use paper towels to press and soak up any moisture from the zucchini.

3. In a medium mixing bowl, combine the ricotta, 1 cup of mozzarella cheese, the egg, olive oil, Italian seasoning, garlic powder, and onion, stirring with a spatula until well combined.

4. Spread 1 cup of marinara sauce on the bottom of the prepared baking dish.

5. Place a layer of zucchini strips on the sauce, followed by a layer of the ricotta cheese mixture. Repeat these layers until the dish is filled to the top. Sprinkle the remaining 1 cup of mozzarella cheese on top.

6. Bake for 35 to 45 minutes, or until the cheese is brown and the sauce is bubbling.

MIX IT UP: If you are not a fan of zucchini, you can use eggplant layers instead for a strikingly similar result! Or you can go all out and use both zucchini and eggplant for a nice variety of nutritious vegetables.

EGGPLANT-CHICKPEA RICE

NUT-FREE, SOY-FREE
SERVES: 4 • **PREP TIME:** 20 minutes • **COOK TIME:** 50 minutes

Another Greek-inspired recipe, this eggplant-chickpea rice bowl is a super-satiating meatless meal, and it can be made as either a side or a main dish. I love how the Greek yogurt, dill, and lemon come together to create an easy-to-make tzatziki sauce.

1. On a cutting board, use a chef's knife to slice the eggplant into thin, 1-inch pieces. Place the pieces in a large mixing bowl, and sprinkle them with salt. Let the eggplant sit for 10 to 15 minutes to soak up the salt, or until beads of liquid form on the surface and the vegetable starts to look a little shriveled. The salt removes excess moisture that can create a bitter taste. Pat the eggplant dry with a paper towel.

2. While the eggplant sits, use a paring knife to mince the garlic. Using the chef's knife, halve the lemon, chop the mint, mince the dill, and cut the cucumber into thin slices. Rinse and drain the chickpeas and set aside.

3. Bring a pot of water to a boil, and cook the jasmine rice according to the package directions.

4. Meanwhile, in a nonstick pan over medium heat, heat the olive oil and sauté the garlic for 3 minutes.

1 medium
    eggplant, sliced
Salt, to taste
1 tablespoon olive oil
4 garlic cloves, minced
Juice of 1 lemon
    divided
1 teaspoon dried mint
2 teaspoons minced
    fresh dill
1 cucumber, very
    thinly sliced
1 (15-ounce) can
    chickpeas, rinsed
    and drained
2 cups uncooked
    jasmine rice
½ teaspoon
    dried oregano
Pepper, to taste
2 cups Greek yogurt

Cutting board
Knives (chef's
    and paring)
Large mixing bowl
Measuring cups
    and spoons
Nonstick pan
Paper towel
Pot
Small mixing bowl
Spatula

(CONTINUED)

5. Squeeze out all the juice you can from ½ lemon into the pan, being careful to catch and discard any seeds. Add the eggplant, oregano, mint, and chickpeas, sautéing for about 5 minutes. Using a spatula, stir occasionally, until the eggplant pieces become tender. Season with salt and pepper.

6. In a small mixing bowl, squeeze out all the juice you can from the remaining ½ lemon, being careful to catch and discard any seeds. Add the Greek yogurt, cucumber, and dill, stirring to combine.

7. Transfer the rice to 4 serving bowls. Top with the eggplant and chickpea mixture, then top with the tzatziki sauce.

KITCHEN HACK: Do some advance prep to save time when following longer recipes like this one. For example, you can make the tzatziki (step 6) the night before and store it in the fridge.

MUSHROOM RISOTTO

NUT-FREE, SOY-FREE

SERVES: 4 • **PREP TIME:** 15 minutes • **COOK TIME:** 25 minutes

Risotto is a traditional Italian dish that calls for a very specific method of making the rice requiring a bit of patience when it comes to stirring the pot. The creamy result is oh so worth the extra work.

1. In a small saucepan over medium heat, heat the broth until it comes to a simmer. Lower the heat and keep the broth at a simmer.

2. Meanwhile, on a cutting board, use a paring knife to mince the garlic and dice the shallot and mushrooms.

3. In a pot over medium heat, heat the olive oil and sauté the garlic and shallot for 3 minutes. Add the mushrooms, 1 tablespoon of butter, and thyme, and continue cooking until the mushrooms become tender.

4. Add the uncooked rice to the pan, along with the white wine vinegar and just enough vegetable broth to cover the rice. As you slowly pour the vegetable broth, continually stir the rice with a wooden spoon to help it absorb all the liquid.

5. Continue adding the broth slowly at intervals. A good indicator of when to add more broth is when it becomes totally absorbed into the rice. It should take somewhere between 15 and 25 minutes to use up all the broth.

6. Stir in the Asiago cheese, remaining 1 tablespoon of butter, salt, and pepper, stirring to incorporate well.

7. Remove the risotto from the heat and serve.

6 cups vegetable broth
1 cup uncooked arborio rice
3 garlic cloves, minced
1 shallot, diced
1 pound baby bella mushrooms, diced
1 tablespoon olive oil
2 tablespoons butter, divided
½ tablespoon white wine vinegar
1 teaspoon thyme
1 cup shredded Asiago cheese
Salt and pepper, to taste

Cutting board
Knife (paring)
Large pot
Measuring cups and spoons
Small saucepan
Wooden spoon

THAI LETTUCE CUPS

30-MINUTE MEAL, DAIRY-FREE, NUT-FREE, VEGAN
SERVES: 4 • **PREP TIME:** 10 minutes • **COOK TIME:** 15 minutes

INGREDIENTS

3 tablespoons
  soy sauce
1 tablespoon
  brown sugar
2 teaspoons
  rice vinegar
1 (1-inch) piece fresh
  ginger, peeled
  and minced
2 garlic cloves, minced
1 shallot, diced
Juice of 1 lime
8 ounces white button
  mushrooms,
  chopped
1 celery stalk, chopped
2 cups
  shredded carrots
1 teaspoon sesame oil
4 butter lettuce leaves

TOOLS

Cheese grater
Cutting board
Knives (chef's
  and paring)
Measuring cups
  and spoons
Nonstick pan
Small mixing bowl
Spoon
Spatula or
  wooden spoon

These lettuce cups are so fresh and vibrant that you won't be able to get enough of them. They are dairy-free and super veggie forward, with a sweet and salty sauce that's very easy to make. This crowd-pleasing meal pairs well with stir-fried rice or Miso Bok Choy Soup (page 48).

1. In a small mixing bowl, stir together the soy sauce, brown sugar, and rice vinegar, then set aside.

2. On a cutting board, use a paring knife to peel and mince the ginger and mince the garlic. Use a chef's knife to dice the shallot, halve the lime, and chop the mushrooms and celery stalk. Use a cheese grater to shred the carrots.

3. In a nonstick pan over medium heat, heat the sesame oil and sauté the garlic, shallot, and ginger for 3 minutes, stirring with a spatula or wooden spoon.

4. Add the mushrooms, celery, and carrots, and continue cooking for about 7 to 8 minutes, or until the vegetables become tender.

5. Squeeze out all the juice you can from the lime into the pan. Add the soy sauce mixture, and continue cooking for about 1 more minute.

6. Scoop the vegetable mixture into each butter lettuce leaf on serving plates.

VEGETARIAN JAMBALAYA

DAIRY-FREE, NUT-FREE, SOY-FREE
SERVES: 4 • **PREP TIME:** 10 minutes • **COOK TIME:** 25 minutes

INGREDIENTS

3 cups vegetable broth
1½ cups uncooked
    brown rice
3 garlic cloves, minced
1 tablespoon chopped
    fresh thyme
1 white onion, diced
1 green bell pepper,
    seeded and diced
1 (15-ounce) can diced
    tomatoes, drained
1 (15-ounce) can
    butter beans,
    rinsed and drained
1 tablespoon olive oil
2 teaspoons sriracha
1 teaspoon
    smoked paprika
Salt and pepper,
    to taste

TOOLS

Cutting board
Knives (chef's
    and paring)
Large pot
Measuring cups
    and spoons
Nonstick pan
Wooden spoon

Jambalaya has its origins in French and Spanish cuisines, and when classically made, it typically includes seafood and meat. For this vegetarian-friendly version, we are eliminating all animal proteins and using butter beans instead. It is a lovely weeknight dinner to make in a big pot for your entire family.

1. In a large pot, bring the vegetable broth to a boil, and cook the rice according to the package directions.

2. While the rice cooks, on a cutting board, use a paring knife to mince the garlic and chop the thyme. Use a chef's knife to dice the onion and seed and dice the bell pepper (see Kitchen Hack on page 42). Drain the tomatoes, and rinse and drain the butter beans. Set aside.

3. In a nonstick pan over medium heat, heat the olive oil and sauté the onion, bell pepper, and garlic for 3 minutes.

4. Add the diced tomatoes, and continue cooking for another 5 minutes.

5. Add the cooked rice, sriracha, smoked paprika, thyme, and butter beans, and continue cooking, stirring occasionally with a wooden spoon, for 5 to 7 minutes.

6. Stir the jambalaya well, season with salt and pepper, and serve immediately.

LENTIL VEGGIE TACOS

30-MINUTE MEAL, NUT-FREE, SOY-FREE
SERVES: 4 • **PREP TIME:** 10 minutes • **COOK TIME:** 10 minutes

This is my easiest taco recipe, and I always make it in a flash whenever I am craving a satisfying taco. Instead of beef, we are using lentils, which are one of my favorite legumes. Lentils are also a great source of iron, which helps with energy, athletic performance, and overall health!

1. Bring a pot of water to a boil, and cook the lentils according to the package directions. Once the lentils have finished cooking, set them aside to cool.

2. Meanwhile, on a cutting board, use a paring knife to mince the garlic. Use a chef's knife to dice the onion, halve the lime, and chop the romaine lettuce. Use a serrated knife to dice the tomatoes.

3. In a nonstick pan over medium heat, heat the coconut oil and sauté the garlic and onion for 3 minutes.

4. Squeeze out all the juice you can from the lime into the pan. Add the tomatoes, cooked lentils, adobo seasoning, and chili powder, and cook for about 7 minutes. Stir with a wooden spoon to ensure all the ingredients are mixed well.

5. Spoon the lentil mixture into the taco shells. Top with the chopped romaine, your cheese of choice, and any other toppings you desire, and serve.

3 cups green lentils
1 garlic clove, minced
1 white onion, diced
Juice of 1 lime
2 romaine lettuce
    leaves, chopped
5 small
    tomatoes, diced
1 tablespoon
    coconut oil
1 teaspoon
    adobo seasoning
1 teaspoon
    chili powder
4 taco shells
1 cup shredded
    cheese of choice

Cutting board
Knives (chef's,
    paring, serrated)
Measuring cups
    and spoons
Nonstick pan
Pot
Saucepan
Spoon
Wooden spoon

ASIAGO ORECCHIETTE

NUT-FREE, SOY-FREE
SERVES: 4 • **PREP TIME:** 10 minutes • **COOK TIME:** 25 minutes

INGREDIENTS

2 cups uncooked
    orecchiette pasta
3 garlic cloves, minced
8 ounces mushrooms,
    chopped
3 cups sliced broccolini
2 tablespoons olive oil
1 cup sun-dried
    tomatoes
1 cup arugula
¼ cup heavy
    whipping cream
2 teaspoons Italian
    seasoning, divided
1 cup shredded
    Asiago cheese

TOOLS

Colander
Cutting board
Knives (chef's
    and paring)
Large pot
Measuring cups
    and spoons
Nonstick pan
Spatula

Did you know that *orecchiette* means "little ears" in Italian? Because of its cute name, this little circular pasta is a popular ingredient in many Italian recipes. This recipe makes an ultra-comforting meal, perfect for a weekend evening when you are in the mood to lounge at home or pop in a family movie.

1. Bring a large pot of water to a boil, and cook the orecchiette pasta according to the package directions.
2. While the pasta cooks, on a cutting board, use a paring knife to mince the garlic. Use a chef's knife to chop the mushrooms and slice the broccolini.
3. Drain the cooked pasta in a colander and set aside.
4. In a nonstick pan over medium heat, heat the olive oil and sauté the garlic for 3 minutes.
5. Add 1 teaspoon of Italian seasoning, the mushrooms, and broccolini, and continue cooking for about 7 minutes, or until the vegetables are tender.
6. Add the sun-dried tomatoes, arugula, heavy whipping cream, and the remaining 1 teaspoon of Italian seasoning, stirring together with a spatula and continuing to cook for about 1 minute.

7. Add the cooked pasta and Asiago cheese. Toss all the ingredients together until the pasta becomes evenly coated, about 1 more minute.

INGREDIENT TIP: To ensure that your Asiago cheese is vegetarian friendly, make sure you are reading the label to ensure that the rennet is from a vegetarian source, like microbial rennet. Or you will see the "V" symbol on the packaging to show that it is vegetarian friendly, too. And a side note: If you don't have broccolini on hand, you can definitely use regular broccoli.

STOVETOP RATATOUILLE

DAIRY-FREE, NUT-FREE, VEGAN
SERVES: 4 • **PREP TIME:** 20 minutes • **COOK TIME:** 25 minutes

INGREDIENTS

1 medium
    eggplant, diced
Salt, to taste
4 garlic cloves, minced
1 white onion, diced
1 large zucchini, sliced
1 large red bell pepper,
    seeded and sliced
6 large
    tomatoes, sliced
6 tablespoons olive
    oil, divided
2 teaspoons paprika
2 teaspoons
    Italian seasoning
Pepper, to taste
½ bunch fresh basil

TOOLS

Cast-iron skillet
Cutting board
Knives (chef's, paring,
    and serrated)
Measuring spoons
Paper towel
Spatula

A wonderfully fragrant French recipe, ratatouille is a stew that bursts with produce. In this dish, we are combining the flavors of eggplant, zucchini, tomatoes, and bell pepper in a cast-iron skillet and bathing it all in olive oil and spices. This vegan recipe makes a delicious main dish that can be served with crusty bread.

1. On a cutting board, use a chef's knife to dice the eggplant, and place the pieces on a plate. Sprinkle the pieces with salt. Let the eggplant sit for about 15 minutes, or until beads of liquid form on the surface and the vegetable starts to look a little shriveled. The salt removes excess moisture that can create a bitter taste. Pat the eggplant pieces dry with a paper towel.

2. While the eggplant sits, use a paring knife to mince the garlic. Use a chef's knife to dice the onion, slice the zucchini, and seed and slice the bell pepper (see Kitchen Hack on page 42). Use a serrated knife to slice the tomatoes.

3. In a cast-iron skillet over medium heat, heat 1 tablespoon of olive oil and sauté the garlic and onion for 3 minutes, stirring with a spatula.

4. Add the eggplant and continue sautéing for about 7 minutes, or until the eggplant becomes tender.

5. Add the remaining 5 tablespoons of olive oil, zucchini, bell pepper, and tomatoes, continuing to cook for another 10 minutes.

6. Add the paprika, Italian seasoning, salt, and pepper, sautéing for 1 to 2 more minutes before adding the fresh basil.

7. Toss everything one more time and remove the skillet from the heat. Transfer to a serving dish, and enjoy!

PROVOLONE PORTOBELLO BURGERS

NUT-FREE, SOY-FREE

SERVES: 4 • **PREP TIME:** 10 minutes, plus 15 to 30 minutes to marinate •
COOK TIME: 20 minutes

INGREDIENTS

1 tablespoon olive oil
2 tablespoons
    balsamic vinegar
1 teaspoon
    garlic powder
½ teaspoon oregano
Salt and pepper,
    to taste
½ teaspoon parsley
4 portobello
    mushroom caps
½ red onion, diced
4 whole-wheat buns
4 slices provolone
    cheese

TOOLS

Cast-iron skillet
Cutting board
Knife (paring)
Measuring spoons
Resealable plastic bag
Spatula

If you thought you would miss having burgers as a vegetarian, you definitely won't with this recipe! Portobello mushrooms already have a "meaty" flavor to them, making them the perfect substitution for beef patties. This recipe calls for a handmade marinade that the mushrooms soak up, giving them a really bold flavor. Once marinated, the mushrooms are sautéed and topped with cheese and red onion, creating a satisfying burger experience.

1. In a resealable plastic bag, add the olive oil, balsamic vinegar, garlic powder, oregano, salt, pepper, and parsley. Shake the bag so that the ingredients blend together.

2. Add the mushroom caps to the bag and marinate in the sauce for 15 to 30 minutes.

3. While the mushroom caps marinate, on a cutting board, using a paring knife to dice the red onion and cut the buns in half if they do not come presliced.

4. In a cast-iron skillet over medium heat, sauté the marinated mushrooms for about 5 minutes on each side, using a spatula to flip them over. As you sauté the mushrooms, drizzle any remaining marinade into the skillet for extra flavor. You may have to cook the mushrooms in batches if your pan does not fit all 4 mushrooms.

5. Place a slice of provolone cheese on top of each mushroom, and cook for 1 more minute, or until the cheese melts.

6. Remove the mushrooms and place them on the bottom half of each bun on individual plates.

7. Top the mushrooms with sliced red onion and any other toppings of your choosing. Place the other halves of the buns on top and serve immediately.

MIX IT UP: You have a lot of options when it comes to toppings for your portobello burgers. You can add mayonnaise, avocado, or Guacamole (page 56) if you want to create a creamy taste. You can also add shredded lettuce on top, or pickled jalapeños if you want to add some spice.

SWEET & SALTY VEGETABLE LO MEIN

30-MINUTE MEAL, DAIRY-FREE, NUT-FREE
SERVES: 4 • **PREP TIME:** 10 minutes • **COOK TIME:** 15 minutes

INGREDIENTS

4 tablespoons soy
    sauce, plus more
    to taste
2 tablespoons tamari
1 teaspoon honey
8 ounces uncooked lo
    mein noodles
3 garlic cloves, minced
1 (1-inch) piece ginger,
    peeled and minced
1 cup chopped
    broccoli
1 cup shredded
    cabbage
1 cup shredded carrots
1 tablespoon
    sesame oil
½ cup snow peas

TOOLS

Cast-iron skillet
Cheese grater
Colander
Cutting board
Knives (chef's
    and paring)
Large pot
Measuring cups
    and spoons
Small mixing bowl
Spatula

Lo mein is a delicious Chinese egg noodle recipe. The noodles resemble Italian pasta, but they aren't made from the same ingredients, which gives them a distinct flavor profile. *Lo mein* translates to "tossed noodles," and they are traditionally made in a wok, but we are going to stick with our trusty old cast-iron skillet for this recipe to keep things simple.

1. In a small mixing bowl, whisk together the soy sauce, tamari, and honey. Set aside.

2. Bring a large pot of water to a boil, and cook the lo mein noodles according to the package directions.

3. While the noodles cook, on a cutting board, use a paring knife to mince the garlic and peel and mince the ginger. Use a chef's knife to chop the broccoli and shred the cabbage. Use a cheese grater to shred the carrots.

4. Drain the cooked noodles in a colander and set aside.

5. In a cast-iron skillet over medium heat, heat the sesame oil and sauté the garlic and ginger for 3 minutes, stirring with a spatula.

6. Add the carrots, broccoli, cabbage, and snow peas, and continue cooking for 5 minutes, or until the vegetables become tender.

7. Add the sauce and cooked noodles. Toss everything together to combine, and add additional soy sauce as desired. Serve immediately.

CHEESY STUFFED PEPPERS

GLUTEN-FREE, NUT-FREE, SOY-FREE
SERVES: 4 • **PREP TIME:** 10 minutes • **COOK TIME:** 40 minutes

Who would think that you can get a completely satisfying meal served inside a bell pepper? This hearty recipe calls for a filling blend of quinoa, beans, green olives, tomatoes, and Monterey Jack cheese stuffed inside peppers and baked to perfection.

1. Preheat the oven to 350°F.
2. On a cutting board, use a chef's knife to pierce through the top of each bell pepper, then cut around the stem. Pull out the stem and insides of the peppers to create what will look like pepper bowls.
3. Bring a saucepan of water to a boil, and cook the quinoa according to the package directions.
4. While the quinoa cooks, use a paring knife to mince the garlic. Use a chef's knife to dice the shallot. Drain the tomatoes, rinse and drain the red beans, and set aside.
5. Place the peppers in a baking dish with the cut side facing up.
6. In a large mixing bowl, combine the tomato sauce, Italian seasoning, garlic, ½ cup of cheese, green olives, shallot, tomatoes, red beans, and cooked quinoa, mixing well with a spatula to combine.

4 large sweet bell peppers, seeded
2 cups uncooked quinoa
3 garlic cloves, minced
1 shallot, diced
1 (15-ounce) can diced tomatoes, drained
1 (15-ounce) can red beans, rinsed and drained
1 (15-ounce) can tomato sauce
1 teaspoon Italian seasoning
1 cup shredded Monterey Jack cheese, divided
⅓ cup green olives
Salt and pepper, to taste

Baking dish
Cutting board
Knives (chef's and paring)
Large mixing bowl
Measuring cups and spoons
Saucepan
Spatula

(CONTINUED)

Cheesy Stuffed Peppers CONTINUED

7. Add salt and pepper to taste and mix well. Scoop the quinoa mixture into each stuffed pepper.

8. Top the peppers with the remaining ½ cup of cheese and bake them for 20 minutes, until the peppers are tender and the cheese has browned on top. Let them cool before serving.

KITCHEN HACK: When I know I am going to be making a lot of meals from scratch throughout the week, I will usually batch cook different food groups to cut down on my overall cooking time. To help cut down on the cook time for this recipe, you can make a big batch of quinoa the night before and completely eliminate an entire step!

GNOCCHI IN CREAMY TOMATO SAUCE

30-MINUTE MEAL, NUT-FREE, SOY-FREE
SERVES: 4 • **PREP TIME:** 5 minutes • **COOK TIME:** 20 minutes

Gnocchi is a wonderful potato-based pasta that looks like little dumplings, and when prepared with the right ingredients, it tastes like a dream. The Greek yogurt in this dish gives the sauce a wonderfully creamy taste with hidden protein, and the Italian spices will make you feel like you are eating at a five-star Italian eatery!

1. Bring a pot of water to a boil, sprinkle some salt into the water, and cook the gnocchi until they float to the top. This is how you will know they are done.

2. Meanwhile, on a cutting board, use a paring knife to mince the garlic, dice the onion, and chop the basil. Use a chef's knife to halve a lemon.

3. In a nonstick pan over medium heat, heat the olive oil and sauté the garlic and onion for 3 minutes.

4. Add the tomato sauce, Greek yogurt, Italian seasoning, and juice from half a lemon, cooking and stirring with a spatula for about 20 minutes.

Salt, to taste
1 pound uncooked gnocchi
3 garlic cloves, minced
1 medium onion, diced
¼ cup chopped fresh basil
Juice of ½ lemon
¼ cup olive oil
1 (12-ounce) can tomato sauce
½ cup Greek yogurt
1 tablespoon Italian seasoning
Pepper, to taste

Cutting board
Knives (paring and chef's)
Measuring cups and spoons
Nonstick pan
Pot
Spatula

(CONTINUED)

Gnocchi in Creamy Tomato Sauce CONTINUED

5. Drain the gnocchi in a colander and add to the pan along with the fresh basil. Toss all the ingredients together so that the gnocchi is evenly coated with sauce.

6. Season with salt and pepper, stir to combine, remove from the stovetop, and serve!

INGREDIENT TIP: When cooking gnocchi, it is important to add some salt to the water so that the gnocchi itself gets some flavor. You can also add some extra spice with a few shakes of red pepper flakes or a sprinkle of your favorite salty cheese on top.

DOUBLE BEAN CHILI

DAIRY-FREE, GLUTEN-FREE, NUT-FREE, SOY-FREE, VEGAN
SERVES: 4 • **PREP TIME:** 10 minutes • **COOK TIME:** 30 minutes

Chili is one of my favorite one-pot comfort foods to make because it warms me up whenever I eat it! This is definitely a recipe that can convert a meat lover, since it is so hearty and satisfying. I always love to load up on chili powder and paprika when I make chili, so if you find that you want to add an extra teaspoon of these spices to your chili, feel free!

1. On a cutting board, use a paring knife to dice the red onion, mince the garlic, and chop the celery stalks. Rinse and drain the white beans and pinto beans and set aside.

2. In a large pot over medium heat, heat the olive oil and sauté the onion, garlic, and celery for 3 minutes.

3. Add the tomatoes, chili powder, paprika, and water, cooking for another minute and stirring all the ingredients together with a wooden spoon.

4. Add the beans and bay leaves, and stir well. Bring the pot to a simmer, and maintain the simmer for about 25 minutes, stirring occasionally.

5. Remove the chili from the heat, discard the bay leaves, and serve it immediately.

MIX IT UP: When it comes to toppings, a dollop of sour cream or Greek yogurt is a wonderful, creamy addition to the chili. A sprinkle of cheese and chopped scallions also provide a tasty combination of flavors. Alternately, you can top the chili with avocado, thin tortilla chips, and a squeeze of lime.

1 red onion, diced
4 garlic cloves, minced
2 celery
    stalks, chopped
2 (15-ounce) cans
    white beans, rinsed
    and drained
1 (15-ounce) can
    pinto beans, rinsed
    and drained
2 tablespoons olive oil
1 (28-ounce) can
    diced tomatoes
2 tablespoons
    chili powder
2 teaspoons
    smoked paprika
2 cups water
2 bay leaves

Cutting board
Knife (paring)
Large pot
Measuring cups
    and spoons
Wooden spoon

VEGGIE-STUFFED EGGPLANT

DAIRY-FREE, GLUTEN-FREE, VEGAN

SERVES: 4 • **PREP TIME:** 25 minutes • **COOK TIME:** 30 minutes

INGREDIENTS

1 medium eggplant,
    halved lengthwise
Salt, to taste
1 medium white
    onion, diced
1 zucchini, diced
8 ounces cremini
    mushrooms,
    chopped
2 garlic cloves, minced
½ cup water
½ cup extra virgin
    olive oil
1 teaspoon cumin
1 teaspoon coriander
1 tablespoon parsley
1 tablespoon
    dried mint
Pepper, to taste
Slivered almonds,
    for garnish

TOOLS

Aluminum foil
Baking dish
Cutting board
Knives (chef's
    and paring)
Large pot
Measuring cups
    and spoons
Paper towel
Small bowl
Spatula
Spoon

Once you get the hang of cooking with eggplant, you may find yourself as hooked on it as I am! This vegetable is completely underrated, but it truly tastes amazing—especially when it is prepared with other delicious vegetables and Middle Eastern spices.

1. Preheat the oven to 350°F.

2. On a cutting board, use a chef's knife to cut the eggplant in half lengthwise. Use a spoon to scoop out the flesh into a small bowl. Sprinkle salt on the eggplant flesh and on the eggplant shells. Let them sit for about 15 minutes to soak in the salt, or until beads of liquid form on the surface and the vegetable starts to look a little shriveled. The salt removes excess moisture that can create a bitter taste. Pat the eggplant flesh and shells dry with a paper towel.

3. Use the chef's knife to dice the onion and zucchini and chop the mushrooms. Use a paring knife to mince the garlic.

4. Pour the water in a baking dish, and place the eggplant shells in the dish, cut-side up. Cover the dish with aluminum foil and bake for 15 minutes.

5. Meanwhile, in a large pot over medium heat, heat the olive oil and sauté the garlic and onion for 3 minutes, stirring with a spatula.

6. Add the zucchini, eggplant flesh, and mushrooms to the pot, sautéing for 5 minutes, or until the vegetables become tender.

7. Add the cumin, coriander, parsley, and mint, and cook for another 5 minutes.

8. Remove the baking dish from the oven, and transfer the vegetable filling to each eggplant shell.

9. Place the stuffed eggplants back in the oven for 15 minutes. Remove them when they have browned slightly.

10. Season with salt and pepper, and garnish with slivered almonds. Cut each stuffed eggplant in half and transfer to serving dishes.

DOUBLE CHOCOLATE
RASPBERRY BROWNIES,
PAGE 152

chapter 7
DESSERTS

If you have a sweet tooth, you will love this chapter. It's packed with recipes that will absolutely delight your taste buds. As an added bonus, you'll find that many of the recipes also have a hidden nutritional punch, so there's no need for guilt.

ALMOND APPLE CRISP

GLUTEN-FREE, SOY-FREE

SERVES: 4 • **PREP TIME:** 15 minutes • **COOK TIME:** 45 minutes

INGREDIENTS

Nonstick cooking
    spray
4 red apples, cored
    and sliced
½ cup almond flour
½ teaspoon
    almond extract
½ cup brown sugar
½ cup old-
    fashioned oats
1 teaspoon cinnamon
½ teaspoon nutmeg
5 tablespoons plus
    1 teaspoon butter

TOOLS

Baking dish
Cutting board
Handheld mixer
Knife (paring)
Measuring cups
    and spoons
Medium mixing bowl
Whisk

One of my favorite fall recipes, this easy almond apple crisp is so delightful. It tastes like something your grandma might make, and when it is baking in the oven, the whole kitchen smells amazing. This version uses almond flour instead of pastry flour to make it gluten-free and full of healthy fats. Top it with a scoop of vanilla ice cream for some extra deliciousness.

1. Preheat the oven to 375°F. Grease a baking dish with cooking spray and set aside.

2. On a cutting board, use a paring knife to core and slice the apples. Set aside.

3. In a medium mixing bowl, whisk together the almond flour, almond extract, sugar, oats, cinnamon, and nutmeg.

4. Add the butter and use a handheld mixer to beat the ingredients together until the mixture looks coarse and crunchy.

5. Place the apple slices evenly in the prepared baking dish and sprinkle the flour mixture all over the slices.

6. Bake for 45 minutes, or until the top of the crumble looks golden brown. Let it cool for 20 minutes before serving.

MIX IT UP: Don't worry if you don't have almond flour on hand. Any type of flour—from whole-wheat to pastry flour—will still make this apple crumble dessert taste fantastic. You can also leave out the oats, but I personally love having that extra crunch.

NO-BAKE CHOCOLATE PEANUT BUTTER TRUFFLES

DAIRY-FREE, GLUTEN-FREE, SOY-FREE

MAKES: About 10 truffles (2 truffles per serving) • **PREP TIME:** 10 minutes • **CHILL TIME:** 30 minutes

My favorite dessert recipes are those that do not require any baking. This one is prepared in one mixing bowl, then simply transferred over to an ice cube tray to set. These peanut butter chocolate truffles are extremely creamy and rich, so you will be satisfied with just one bite.

3 tablespoons melted coconut oil
¼ cup peanut butter
1 teaspoon vanilla extract
2 tablespoons cocoa powder
1 tablespoon honey

Handheld mixer
Ice cube tray
Measuring cups and spoons
Medium mixing bowl
Microwave-safe bowl
Spoon

1. In a microwave-safe bowl, heat the coconut oil in the microwave for about 30 seconds, or until melted.

2. In a medium mixing bowl, use a handheld mixer on low speed to blend together the coconut oil, peanut butter, vanilla extract, cocoa powder, and honey until smooth.

3. Scoop out spoonfuls of the mixture and place them in an ice cube tray, until you have used all the mixture.

4. Transfer the tray to the freezer for about 30 minutes to set before serving.

INGREDIENT TIP: You should always store these chocolate truffles in the refrigerator. When coconut oil is in a warm environment, it naturally becomes liquid. Keeping your truffles chilled will ensure they remain solid.

NO-BAKE RASPBERRY CHEESECAKE BITES

NUT-FREE

MAKES: About 20 bites (2 bites per serving) • **PREP TIME:** 15 minutes •
CHILL TIME: 1 hour or overnight

INGREDIENTS

½ cup crushed
    graham crackers
4 tablespoons
    butter, melted
2¼ cups granulated
    sugar, divided
½ teaspoon
    vanilla extract
½ cup fresh
    raspberries
8 ounces cream
    cheese, softened
¼ cup chocolate chips

TOOLS

Baking sheet
Handheld mixer
Knife (chef's)
Large mixing bowl
Microwave-safe bowl
Spatula
Spoon
Parchment paper

Another fabulous no-bake dessert, these cheesecake bites are made with fresh raspberries, graham crackers, and chocolate chips sprinkled on top. The graham cracker crust is rich, buttery, and sweet, whereas the cheesecake layer is light and fluffy. The chocolate chips give each bite extra texture. This batch makes about 20 bites, depending on the size (try not to make the bites *too* big, because sharing is caring!).

1. In a large mixing bowl, crush the graham crackers with a spoon.

2. In a microwave-safe bowl, heat the butter in the microwave for 10 to 20 seconds, or until it has fully liquified.

3. Add 2 cups of sugar and the butter to the mixing bowl, stirring with a spatula to combine.

4. Line a baking sheet with parchment paper and transfer the graham cracker mixture onto it, then press it down to make a thin crust. Transfer the crust to the freezer to set.

5. Meanwhile, in the same bowl used to make the crust, combine the remaining ¼ cup of sugar, vanilla extract, raspberries, and cream cheese, blending with a handheld mixer until smooth.

6. Pour this mixture onto the crust, and smooth it out evenly with a spatula. Top it with the chocolate chips and place back in the freezer for about 1 hour to set (or overnight if you are making it the night before).

7. Once the cheesecake has set, remove it from the freezer, and let it sit for 10 minutes. Use a chef's knife to cut it into squares, and serve. Store leftovers in the freezer.

MIX IT UP: You can use whatever berry you like most for this recipe. Blueberries, strawberries, and blackberries taste just as great in this cheesecake recipe. You can even use berry jam instead spread it on top of the cheesecake layer, rather than blending the fruit in.

CHOCOLATE ZUCCHINI BREAD

GLUTEN-FREE

SERVES: 4 • **PREP TIME:** 15 minutes • **COOK TIME:** 45 minutes

INGREDIENTS

1¼ packed cups
    shredded zucchini
Nonstick
    cooking spray
1¼ cup oat flour
¾ teaspoon
    baking soda
½ cup cocoa powder
¼ teaspoon
    baking powder
1 cup chocolate chips
2 large eggs
¼ cup coconut oil
½ cup brown sugar
¼ cup almond milk

TOOLS

Cheese grater
Cutting board
Fork
Loaf pan
Mixing bowls (2)
Paper towels
Spatula
Whisk

If you are thinking that this sweet, chocolaty bread will taste strange when combined with zucchini, you will be pleasantly surprised. This bread tastes almost like a cake, and you can barely tell that you added any vegetables to it!

1. On a cutting board, use a cheese grater to shred the zucchini, then place the zucchini between a couple of paper towels and press down to soak up any excess moisture. Set it aside.

2. Preheat the oven to 350°F. Grease a loaf pan with cooking spray and set aside.

3. In a mixing bowl, whisk together the flour, baking soda, cocoa powder, baking powder, and chocolate chips.

4. In another mixing bowl, whisk together the eggs, coconut oil, brown sugar, and almond milk. Beat until well blended, then pour this mixture into the bowl with the dry ingredients. Whisk to combine.

5. Fold in the zucchini with a spatula, stirring gently to combine.

6. Transfer the bread mixture into the prepared loaf pan and bake for 45 minutes, or until you can insert a fork in the center and it comes out clean. If the fork does not come out clean after 45 minutes, you may need to continue to bake it longer, checking it frequently.

7. Once your bread is baked, allow it to cool before serving.

GREEK YOGURT LEMON TART BARS

GLUTEN-FREE, SOY-FREE

MAKES: About 12 bars (3 bars per serving) • **PREP TIME:** 15 minutes •
COOK TIME: 50 minutes

This lemon tart bar recipe is citrusy and sweet all in one. I always make these during the spring, since the flavor reminds me of fresh flowers and warm weather. I also love the fact that this recipe uses honey for sweetness instead of refined sugar.

1 cup oat flour, plus
    2 tablespoons,
    divided
⅓ cup coconut oil
¼ teaspoon salt
½ teaspoon
    vanilla extract
⅓ cup honey,
    plus ¼ cup
Juice of 4 lemons
3 eggs
1 cup Greek yogurt

Baking dish
Cutting board
Handheld mixer
Knife (chef's)
Measuring cups
    and spoons
Medium mixing bowl
Parchment paper
Small mixing bowl
Spatula
Spoon

1. Preheat the oven to 350°F. Line a baking dish with parchment paper and set aside.

2. In a small mixing bowl, combine 1 cup of oat flour, the coconut oil, salt, vanilla extract, and ⅓ cup of honey, stirring well with a spatula.

3. Transfer the dough to the prepared baking dish, and spread it evenly on the bottom of the dish with a spoon.

4. Bake the crust for 20 minutes, then set it aside to cool.

5. Meanwhile, on a cutting board, use a chef's knife to halve the lemons. Squeeze out all the juice you can from the lemons into a medium mixing bowl, being careful to catch and discard any seeds. Add the remaining ¼ cup of honey, remaining oat flour, the eggs, and Greek yogurt, and blend well with a handheld mixer.

(CONTINUED)

6. Top the crust in the baking dish with the lemon filling, spreading it around to get an even layer. Place the dish back in the oven for 30 minutes.

7. Remove from the oven and set aside to cool completely. Use a chef's knife to cut into bars, serve, and enjoy!

INGREDIENT TIP: When making dessert recipes with lemons, it can be tricky to tell how much juice you are getting from one lemon. From experience, I have always squeezed out 2 tablespoons from one average-size lemon. I never really use a citrus squeezer, but if you have one on hand, this can help you get as much juice from your lemons as possible.

CHOCOLATE BANANA CAKE

NUT-FREE

SERVES: 6 • **PREP TIME:** 15 minutes • **BAKE TIME:** 25 minutes

INGREDIENTS

Nonstick cooking
    spray
3 medium ripe
    bananas
½ cup brown sugar
2 teaspoons vanilla
    extract
½ cup applesauce
1½ cups wheat flour
⅓ cup cocoa powder
1 teaspoon baking
    soda
Pinch salt
⅓ cup chocolate chips

TOOLS

Baking dish
Fork
Measuring cups
    and spoons
Medium mixing
    bowls (2)
Whisk

This cake recipe is a bit different from traditional cake recipes, as it doesn't call for eggs, oil, or butter! What is the secret, you ask? Applesauce. Between the applesauce and bananas, this cake turns out ultramoist and extra chocolaty without being greasy. I don't add frosting, since I think it tastes great without it, but you can always spread some premade frosting on top if you so choose.

1. Preheat the oven to 350°F. Grease a baking dish with cooking spray and set aside.

2. In a medium mixing bowl, mash the bananas and sugar together with a fork. Add the vanilla and applesauce and mix well.

3. In another medium mixing bowl, whisk together the wheat flour, cocoa powder, baking soda, and salt.

4. Add the flour mixture to the banana mixture and whisk together until all the ingredients are well combined. If the batter seems too thick, you can add up to ⅓ cup water to thin it out.

5. Add the chocolate chips to the batter, stirring gently to incorporate them.

6. Transfer the batter to the prepared baking dish and bake for 25 minutes, or until a fork inserted in the center comes out clean.

ALMOND BLUEBERRY CRISP

DAIRY-FREE, GLUTEN-FREE, VEGAN
SERVES: 4 • **PREP TIME:** 15 minutes • **COOK TIME:** 40 minutes

Similar to Almond Apple Crisp (page 134), this dessert is a fruit-forward yet decadent option. It tastes delicious topped with ice cream and is a perfect party pleaser for family gatherings. I especially like this dessert recipe for Sunday brunch gatherings, since it is not very heavy, so you won't end up in a food coma after eating it.

1. Preheat the oven to 350°F. Grease a baking dish with cooking spray and set aside.

2. On a cutting board, use a chef's knife to halve the lemon.

3. Squeeze out as much juice as you can from the lemon into a medium mixing bowl, being careful to catch and discard any seeds. Add the blueberries, almond extract, and 2 tablespoons of brown sugar. Mix well with a spatula to combine.

4. Transfer the blueberry mixture to the prepared baking dish.

5. In the same bowl, whisk together the oats, almond flour, coconut oil, the remaining 2 tablespoons of brown sugar, and cinnamon.

6. Spread the topping over the blueberries in the baking dish.

7. Bake for 40 minutes, or until the top is golden and crisp. Let cool before serving.

INGREDIENT TIP: This recipe also tastes great with crushed pecans or slivered almonds on top. If you are not a fan of nuts, stick with the oatmeal topping.

Nonstick cooking
    spray
Juice of 1 lemon
3½ cups frozen
    blueberries
½ teaspoon
    almond extract
4 tablespoons brown
    sugar, divided
1 cup old-
    fashioned oats
2 tablespoons
    almond flour
2 tablespoons
    coconut oil
1 teaspoon cinnamon

Baking dish
Cutting board
Knife (chef's)
Measuring cups
    and spoons
Medium mixing bowl
Spatula
Whisk

STRAWBERRY BLONDIES

GLUTEN-FREE, SOY-FREE

MAKES: About 12 bars (3 bars per serving) • **PREP TIME:** 15 minutes •
COOK TIME: 30 minutes

INGREDIENTS

1 cup fresh
     strawberries, sliced
Juice of 1 lemon
¾ cup brown sugar
8 tablespoons
     (1 stick) butter
1 egg
1 cup almond flour
½ teaspoon salt
½ teaspoon
     baking powder
1 tablespoon
     strawberry jam

TOOLS

Baking dish
Cutting board
Fork
Handheld mixer
Knives (chef's, paring,
     and table)
Measuring cups
     and spoons
Medium mixing
     bowls (2)
Parchment paper
Spatula
Whisk

These strawberry blondies taste like a mix between dense cookies and cake. But what exactly are "blondies"? They are pretty much the nonchocolate version of brownies. They have some of the same ingredients but don't use chocolate. This blondie recipe focuses on celebrating the strawberry, which, when combined with lemon juice, creates a light and tangy flavor.

1. Preheat the oven to 350°F. Line a baking dish with parchment paper and set aside.

2. On a cutting board, use a paring knife to slice the strawberries, and use a chef's knife to halve the lemon. Set aside.

3. In a medium mixing bowl, use a handheld mixer to beat together the sugar and butter until they are fluffy. Add the egg and continue beating the mixture together.

4. In another medium mixing bowl, whisk together the flour, salt, and baking powder.

5. Transfer the dry ingredients to the bowl containing the wet ingredients and combine using the mixer. Squeeze out as much juice as you can from the lemon into the bowl, being careful to catch and discard any seeds. Mix for another 1 to 2 minutes to combine.

6. Use a spatula to fold in the sliced strawberries and spread the mixture in the prepared baking dish so that it covers the entire bottom of the dish.

7. Bake for 30 minutes, or until a fork inserted into the center comes out clean.

8. Remove the blondies from the oven, and use a table knife to spread the strawberry jam on top. Use a chef's knife to cut them into bars, and enjoy.

AVOCADO CHOCOLATE PUDDING

DAIRY-FREE, GLUTEN-FREE, SOY-FREE, VEGAN
SERVES: 4 • **PREP TIME:** 10 minutes • **CHILL TIME:** 30 minutes

INGREDIENTS

2 ripe avocados,
    peeled and pitted
¼ cup almond milk
½ cup cocoa powder
1 teaspoon
    vanilla extract
¼ cup maple syrup

TOOLS

Blender
Jar
Knife (chef's)
Measuring cups
    and spoons
Spoon

Even though the total time to make this pudding recipe is 40 minutes, it calls for just 10 minutes or less of hands-on work! This recipe is one of my favorite healthier desserts. Another sneaky veggie-based dessert, this one blends avocado with almond milk and cocoa powder to create a creamy texture. This is the perfect vegan alternative to traditional pudding without sacrificing the silky texture or flavor of the real thing.

1. On a cutting board, use a chef's knife to peel and pit the avocados (see Kitchen Hack on page 19). Use a spoon to remove the flesh.

2. In a blender, combine the avocado flesh, almond milk, cocoa powder, vanilla extract, and maple syrup, and blend until smooth.

3. Transfer the pudding to a jar and let it chill in the refrigerator for 30 minutes before serving.

BANANA COCONUT ICE CREAM

30-MINUTE MEAL, DAIRY-FREE, GLUTEN-FREE, SOY-FREE, VEGAN
SERVES: 4 • **PREP TIME:** 10 minutes

Did you know that you can make vegan ice cream using bananas? By blending frozen bananas in a blender with coconut milk, you can replicate the taste and texture of soft-serve ice cream. I started making this recipe almost nightly when I was craving something sweet but didn't want to overindulge. It is the perfect sweet-tooth satisfier without any added sugars, flours, or butter.

1. On a cutting board, use a chef's knife to chop the frozen bananas, then place them in a blender with the coconut milk and salt.

2. Blend all the ingredients together until smooth, and serve immediately!

MIX IT UP: If the taste of bananas is not your favorite, you can add all sorts of ingredients to this ice cream recipe to make it taste just how you want. Sometimes, I like adding a scoop of peanut butter to give it nutty flavor, or loading up on the cocoa powder to transform it into chocolate ice cream.

4 frozen bananas, chopped
½ cup full-fat coconut milk
Pinch salt

Blender
Cutting board
Knife (chef's)
Measuring cups

PEPPERMINT CHOCOLATE SQUARES

GLUTEN-FREE

MAKES: About 10 squares (2 squares per serving) •
PREP TIME: 1 hour 15 minutes • **CHILL TIME:** 15 to 30 minutes

This is the ultimate homemade version of peppermint patties, but in a bar! Another great no-bake dessert recipe, this one calls for cashews as the peppermint base, mixed with peppermint extract and brown sugar to give it delicious sweetness.

INGREDIENTS

½ cup raw cashews, soaked
½ cup coconut oil, divided
2 tablespoons brown sugar
1 teaspoon peppermint extract
¼ cup coconut milk
1 cup chocolate chips

TOOLS

Baking dish
Colander
Measuring cups and spoons
Mixing bowl
Parchment paper
Small saucepan or microwave-safe bowl
Spoon

1. In a mixing bowl full of water, soak the cashews for 1 hour to tenderize. After an hour, drain and rinse the cashews in a colander.

2. In a blender, combine the cashews, ¼ cup of coconut oil, the brown sugar, peppermint extract, and coconut milk. Blend until mixed together well.

3. Line a shallow baking dish with parchment paper, and transfer the cashew blend to it, spreading the mixture evenly across the bottom with a spoon.

4. Heat the chocolate chips in a small saucepan on the stove or in a microwave-safe bowl in the microwave until they are completely melted. Pour the chocolate over the cashew layer.

5. Place the baking dish in the freezer and let it set for 15 to 30 minutes. Use a chef's knife to cut into bars, and enjoy.

KITCHEN HACK: If you know you are going to make this recipe, you can soak the cashews overnight in the fridge to save on time.

PEANUT BUTTER MOUSSE

30-MINUTE MEAL, GLUTEN-FREE, SOY-FREE
SERVES: 4 • **PREP TIME:** 5 minutes • **CHILL TIME:** 15 minutes

This peanut butter mousse is whipped up with a hand-held mixer and requires just 5 minutes of hands-on time. If you are a fan of peanut butter in general, you will absolutely love this sweet treat. I really like the fact that you are getting healthy fats from the coconut milk and protein from the peanut butter in this dessert recipe. For a slightly different taste, try honey instead of brown sugar.

1 (15-ounce) can
    coconut milk
½ cup creamy
    peanut butter
3 ounces cream
    cheese, softened
2 tablespoons
    brown sugar
½ teaspoon
    vanilla extract
Whipped cream,
    for garnish

Measuring cups
    and spoons
Medium mixing bowl
Handheld mixer

1. In a medium mixing bowl, combine the coconut milk, peanut butter, cream cheese, sugar, and vanilla extract. Use a handheld mixer to whip all the ingredients on low speed until they are well combined.
2. Transfer the mixture to serving bowls, then chill in the refrigerator for 15 minutes.
3. Garnish each bowl with a dollop of whipped cream, and serve.

GREEK YOGURT VANILLA CUPCAKES

NUT-FREE, SOY-FREE

MAKES: 10 cupcakes (1 cupcake per serving) • **PREP TIME:** 15 minutes •
COOK TIME: 25 minutes

INGREDIENTS

6 tablespoons
     (¾ stick) butter
1 cup brown sugar
½ cup Greek yogurt
1 teaspoon vanilla
     extract
2 eggs
2 cups pastry flour
1 teaspoon baking
     powder
½ teaspoon
     baking soda
¼ teaspoon salt
1 (1-pound) tub
     store-bought
     frosting

TOOLS

Cupcake liners
Fork
Handheld mixer
Measuring cups
     and spoons
Medium mixing
     bowls (2)
Muffin tin (with at least
     10 cups)
Spoon
Whisk

These Greek yogurt vanilla cupcakes are extra special because they can be customized based on what flavor frosting you choose. I enjoy making cupcakes from scratch and adding my favorite store-bought frosting to top it off. This way, you can be creative with your flavors. I also love adding Greek yogurt to my recipes because it creates a slightly different taste and also helps activate the baking soda, which makes baked goods even fluffier.

1. Preheat the oven to 350°F. Place 10 cupcake liners in a muffin tin and set aside.

2. In a medium mixing bowl, use a handheld mixer to beat together the butter and sugar until they look fluffy.

3. Add the yogurt, vanilla extract, and eggs, and continue beating so they are well combined.

4. In a separate medium mixing bowl, whisk together the flour, baking powder, baking soda, and salt.

5. Transfer the dry ingredients to the bowl containing the wet ingredients and mix together with the handheld mixer.

6. Spoon the batter into each cupcake liner in the prepared tin. Make sure you don't fill the liners completely, as the batter will rise in the oven. Bake the cupcakes for 25 minutes, or until you can insert a fork in the center and it comes out clean.

7. Remove the tin from the oven and let the cupcakes cool. Spread your frosting of choice on top, and serve.

DID YOU KNOW? By adding Greek yogurt to your cupcakes, you are creating an extra-moist and delicious texture as well as adding protein and calcium to each bite.

DOUBLE CHOCOLATE RASPBERRY BROWNIES

NUT-FREE

MAKES: About 10 brownies (2 brownies per serving) •
PREP TIME: 15 minutes • **COOK TIME:** 20 minutes

INGREDIENTS

Nonstick
    cooking spray
½ cup chopped
    chocolate bar
¼ cup coconut oil
2 eggs
¾ cup brown sugar
1 cup all-purpose flour
⅓ cup cocoa powder
¼ teaspoon
    baking powder
¼ teaspoon salt
½ cup chocolate chips
½ cup freeze-dried
    raspberries

TOOLS

Baking dish
Cutting board
Fork
Handheld mixer
Knife (chef's)
Measuring cups
    and spoons
Medium mixing bowl
Microwave-safe bowl
Spatula

These brownies have double the chocolate because we are blending cocoa powder and solid chocolate together! Each bite is dense, chewy, and oh so sweet. A scrumptious blend of chocolate chips and raspberries gives a bit of textural variety. I love making these brownies when celebrating a birthday and sometimes indulge in these instead of cake. But beware. You will have to refrain from eating all the batter.

1. Preheat the oven to 350°F. Grease a baking dish with cooking spray and set aside.

2. On a cutting board, use a chef's knife to chop the chocolate bar. In a microwave-safe bowl, heat the chocolate bar pieces and coconut oil (if it is solid) in the microwave for 30 seconds, or until melted, then set it aside.

3. In a medium mixing bowl, use a handheld mixer on low speed to combine the eggs and sugar together until well blended. Add the melted chocolate and coconut oil to the bowl, and slowly blend together.

4. Add the flour, cocoa powder, baking powder, and salt to the bowl, and continue blending the ingredients together on low speed until completely smooth.

5. Stir in the chocolate chips with a spatula, then transfer the mixture to the prepared baking dish. Smooth out the mixture so that it covers the entire bottom of the dish, then sprinkle the freeze-dried berries on top.

6. Bake for 20 minutes, or until a fork inserted in the center comes out clean.

7. Allow the brownies to cool before cutting and serving.

US Standard	US Standard (ounces)	Metric (approximate)
2 tablespoons	1 fl. oz.	30 mL
¼ cup	2 fl. oz.	60 mL
½ cup	4 fl. oz.	120 mL
1 cup	8 fl. oz.	240 mL
1½ cups	12 fl. oz.	355 mL
2 cups or 1 pint	16 fl. oz.	475 mL
4 cups or 1 quart	32 fl. oz.	1 L
1 gallon	128 fl. oz.	4 L

Fahrenheit	Celsius (approximate)
250°F	120°C
300°F	150°C
325°F	165°C
350°F	180°C
375°F	190°C
400°F	200°C
425°F	220°C
450°F	230°C

US Standard	Metric (approximate)
⅛ teaspoon	0.5 mL
¼ teaspoon	1 mL
½ teaspoon	2 mL
¾ teaspoon	4 mL
1 teaspoon	5 mL
1 tablespoon	15 mL
¼ cup	59 mL
⅓ cup	79 mL
½ cup	118 mL
⅔ cup	156 mL
¾ cup	177 mL
1 cup	235 mL
2 cups or 1 pint	475 mL
3 cups	700 mL
4 cups or 1 quart	1 L

US Standard	Metric (approximate)
½ ounce	15 g
1 ounce	30 g
2 ounces	60 g
4 ounces	115 g
8 ounces	225 g
12 ounces	340 g
16 ounces or 1 pound	455 g

INDEX

ACKNOWEDGMENTS

I HAVE TO START BY THANKING MY PARENTS FOR RAISING ME TO constantly feel empowered to embark on whichever journey *I chose*, and for cheering me on along the way, especially in my career pursuits, which led me to write this book. I want to thank my husband, Ivan, for supporting me in so many ways. From inspiring me with his delectable home-cooking skills to keeping our son busy on the weekends so I could finish this book, he played a major role in the completion of this project. I also want to give a huge thanks to the entire team at Callisto Media for believing in me and my work. This team has made the writing process enjoyable and manageable, and the support they've given me along the way is more than I could dream of from a publishing partner.

SARAH BAKER is a certified plant-based-nutrition consultant, certified holistic health coach, certified meditation teacher, postpartum doula, and TV wellness correspondent. She is the founder of the multimedia platform BalancedBabe.com and host of *The Balanced Babe Podcast.* In between working with clients and creating content for her podcast, you can also find her on various Chicago morning shows contributing healthy cooking and wellness tips. Sarah's passion is to educate and help her clients and subscribers integrate easy healthy eating and wellness practices that are approachable, enjoyable, and most of all, sustainable! You can also get daily education from her Instagram @Balanced_Babe.

CPSIA information can be obtained
at www.ICGtesting.com
Printed in the USA
LVHW070200220420
654208LV00013B/263